DOCTOR · WHO

ALIENS AND ENEMIES

BY JUSTIN RICHARDS

BBC
BOOKS

Published by BBC Books, BBC Worldwide Ltd, 80 Wood Lane, London W12 0TT

First published 2006. Reprinted 2006 (five times), 2008

ISBN-13: 978 0 563 48646 6

ISBN-10: 0 563 48646 5

Commissioning Editor: Stuart Cooper
Project Editor: Vicki Vrint
Creative Director: Justin Richards
Design and Cover Design: Lee Binding
Production Controller: Peter Hunt

Doctor Who is a BBC Wales production for BBC ONE. Executive Producers: Russell T Davies and Julie Gardner. Producer: Phil Collinson.

Printed and bound by Firmengruppe APPL, aprinta druck, Wemding, Germany. Colour separations by Dot Gradations, Wickford, England.

BBC Books would like to thank the following for providing photographs and for permission to reproduce copyright material. While every effort has been made to trace and acknowledge all copyright holders, we would like to apologise should there have been any errors or omissions. All images copyright © BBC, except:

pages 12 (top), 13 (top and Clockwork Robot mechanism), 18 (bottom left), 26 (bottom left), 58 (bottom right), 60 (bottom right) and 80 (top right) the Braxiatek Collection

page 27 (top right) courtesy of Steve Cambden

page 68 (bottom left) Charlie Lumm

pages 84 (main), 86 (top right and bottom) and 87 (top and bottom) Tony Cornell

page 93 (main) Hulton Archive/Getty Images

All production designs and storyboards are reproduced courtesy of the Doctor Who Art Department. Images on pages 19 (bottom right), 54, 56, 80 (bottom left) and 81 (top right) courtesy of Millennium FX.

All Computer Generated Imagery courtesy of The Mill, including main images on pages 40, 43, 46, 62, 88 and design on page 91.

With additional thanks to:

James Carter   Ian Grutchfield   Brian Minchin   Paul Vanezis
Stephen Cole   Clayton Hickman and all at   Steven Moffat
Paul Cornell   Doctor Who Magazine   Helen Raynor
Russell T Davies   David J. Howe   Edward Russell
Jacqueline Farrow   Gwenllian Llwyd   Matthew Savage
Cameron Fitch   Tom MacRae   Edward Thomas
Neill Gorton   The Mill   Mike Tucker

CONTENTS

ALIENS AND ENEMIES

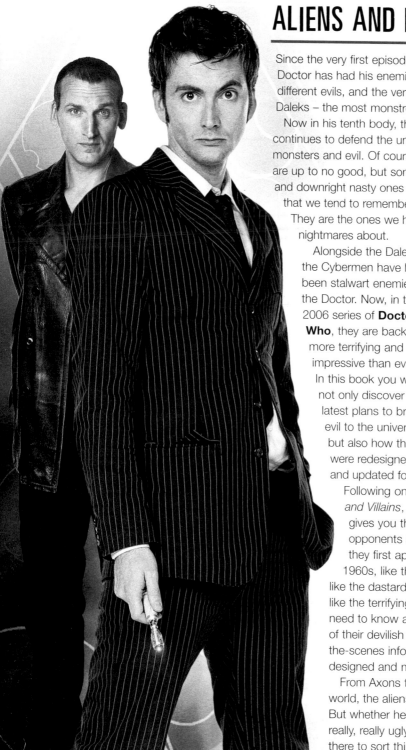

Since the very first episode of **Doctor Who**, way back in 1963, the Doctor has had his enemies. Over the years he has battled many different evils, and the very first aliens he encountered were the Daleks – the most monstrous of all his intergalactic foes.

Now in his tenth body, the Doctor, along with his friend Rose, continues to defend the universe – to defend *us* – from aliens and monsters and evil. Of course, not all the aliens the Doctor meets are up to no good, but somehow it's the unpleasant, monstrous and downright nasty ones that we tend to remember. They are the ones we have nightmares about.

Alongside the Daleks, the Cybermen have long been stalwart enemies of the Doctor. Now, in the 2006 series of **Doctor Who**, they are back – more terrifying and impressive than ever. In this book you will not only discover their latest plans to bring evil to the universe, but also how they were redesigned and updated for a twenty-first-century television audience.

Following on from its companion volume – Monsters and Villains, published in 2005 – Aliens and Enemies gives you the low-down on the Doctor's latest opponents as well as some of his older foes. Whether they first appeared on our television screens in the 1960s, like the dreaded Weed Creature; in the 1970s, like the dastardly time-criminal Magnus Greel; or in 2006, like the terrifying Clockwork Robots, you'll find all you need to know about them in this book. It includes details of their devilish plots and terrible weapons, and behind-the-scenes information about how the creatures were designed and made.

From Axons to Zarbi, from New Earth to our own world, the aliens and enemies of the Doctor are coming. But whether he's faced with the good, the bad or the really, really ugly, we know that the Doctor will always be there to sort things out.

THE CHANGING FACE OF DOCTOR WHO

At the end of *The Parting of the Ways*, the Doctor *changed*. Having saved Rose by taking from her the burning, destructive energies of the Time Vortex, the Doctor was forced to regenerate. He described it as a Time Lord trick to cheat death – a way of saving himself from being consumed by the Time Vortex forces. As Rose watched in amazement, the Doctor was engulfed in a fierce fiery light, and when it faded … a new Doctor was waiting for her – new face, new body, new personality. But underneath it all, he is still the same man: Time's Champion, and Defender of the Earth…

In fact, the new Doctor is the tenth incarnation of the Time Lord. In this book you will meet many of his former selves: the crotchety old man who first appeared on our televisions in the 1960s; the younger, more humorous Second Doctor; the Third Doctor, an action hero banished to Earth in our time… The Fourth Doctor was a larger-than-life wanderer, while the Fifth was a younger, more conventional hero. The Sixth Doctor was bombastic and theatrical, whereas the Seventh was an eccentric. The Eighth Doctor was a young, dashing hero whose ultimate fate remains a mystery.

With the Ninth Doctor's arrival on our screens in 2005, we learned of the terrible Time War – and witnessed its ultimate end. Now the Tenth Doctor is here to battle the monsters, to keep us safe – to protect us from the aliens and enemies…

THE AXONS

The Axons are semi-humanoid manifestations of a composite creature – Axos – a space parasite that feeds on the energy of the planets it visits, destroying them in the process. At first the Axons appear to be beautiful, benevolent gold-skinned humanoids (below right), but in fact they are terrifying, tentacled monsters in disguise (below left). The Axons are immune to bullets and can kill at a touch. They absorb energy and transmit it back to Axos – one Axon is able to transfer the entire output of a nuclear reactor.

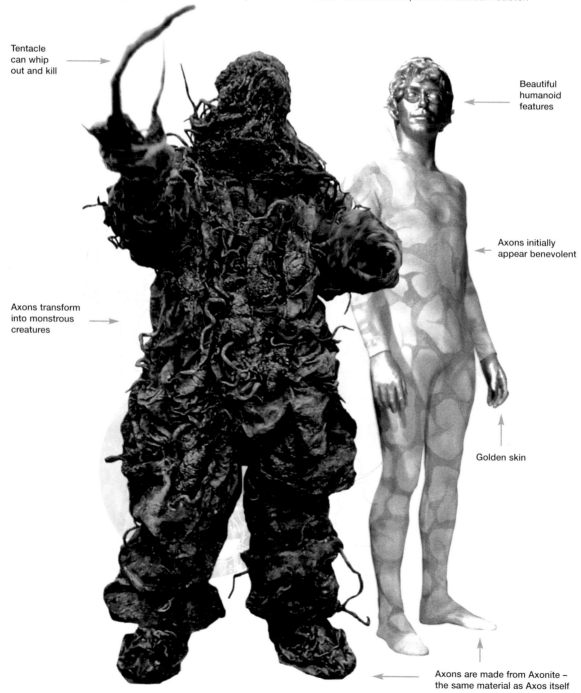

Tentacle can whip out and kill

Axons transform into monstrous creatures

Beautiful humanoid features

Axons initially appear benevolent

Golden skin

Axons are made from Axonite – the same material as Axos itself

The Doctor and the Master work together against the Axons.

THE CLAWS OF AXOS

An organic alien ship lands on Earth, and the friendly humanoid aliens offer Axonite as a gift in return for refuge, claiming their planet was destroyed by a solar flare. But the ship, its occupant, and Axonite are all a single creature that plans to feed on Earth's energy. It starts to absorb energy from the reactor of the Nuton National Power Complex.

As the Axons are revealed to be grotesque, tentacled creatures, the Doctor and UNIT are forced into an uneasy alliance with the Master, a renegade Time Lord who has led Axos to Earth. The Doctor offers to give Axos time-travel technology, but tricks it into becoming trapped in a time loop – travelling forever through a never-ending figure-of-eight in time.

Written by
Bob Baker and Dave Martin
Featuring
the Third Doctor,
UNIT and Jo
First broadcast
13 March 1971 –
3 April 1971
4 episodes

AXONITE

Axonite, Axos and the Axons are a single entity. Axonite can absorb, convert, transmit and programme all forms of energy. The Axons describe it as 'a thinking molecule. It uses the energy it absorbs not only to copy but to recreate and restructure any given substance.' Axos offers it as a gift, copying and enlarging a frog to show how Axonite can provide unlimited food and power.

In fact, once distributed round the world, Axonite will absorb the Earth's energy to feed Axos: 'All things must die … Axos merely hastens the process…'

CREATING THE AXONS

Writers Bob Baker and Dave Martin were invited to write a **Doctor Who** story after submitting a comedy script to the BBC. Their outline, titled *The Gift*, included a creature that was all brain and looked like a giant skull landing in Hyde Park in London. Eventually the story – for a while called *The Vampire From Space* – became less 'epic' and more affordable for the BBC's budget.

The Axons were designed to resemble the interior of Axos, which was organic. Some of the costumes were 'blobby' while others were more tentacled. In fact, the costumes were so organic that costume designer Barbara Lane re-used one, spayed green, as an alien plant, the Krynoid, in the 1976 Fourth Doctor story *The Seeds of Doom*.

THE CLOCKWORK ROBOTS

The Clockwork Robots are responsible for the maintenance and repair of the spaceship the SS *Madame de Pompadour*. The Clockwork Woman shown here is actually Repair Droid 7. The droids are operated by clockwork so that they will work even in the event of a total power failure.

When the ship breaks down catastrophically and suffers 82 per cent systems failure in an ion storm, the droids attempt to repair it. They are programmed to do this in any way they can – even if it means using the crew and passengers as spare parts.

Searching for Reinette – the real Madame de Pompadour – in eighteenth-century France, the droids disguise themselves in contemporary clothing and wigs, and wear ornate masks as if for a masked ball.

Mask and wig cover main clockwork mechanism

Gloves cover clockwork 'hands' with replaceable tool attachments

Repair Droid 7

Clockwork body of droid covered by ball gown or other contemporary clothing

The Clockwork Robots with Reinette at the ball.

GIRL IN THE FIREPLACE

The Doctor, Rose and Mickey find themselves on a damaged spaceship in the fifty-first century, which is linked through 'time windows' to eighteenth-century France. Using the windows, the Doctor meets Reinette and finds she is being menaced by Clockwork Robots. These are repair droids from the ship, who have been trying to get it working again using any spare components they can find – including the crew.

The Doctor visits Reinette several times and they form a close friendship. But can he prevent the robots from using her head to repair the ship? With Rose and Mickey about to be used for spare parts, it is up to the Doctor and his new friend Arthur – a horse – to save the day.

Written by
Steven Moffat
Featuring
the Tenth Doctor,
Rose and Mickey
First broadcast
spring 2006
1 episode

REINETTE

Jeanne-Antionette Poisson was born on 29 December 1721. At the age of nine, her mother took her to a fortune teller, who told the girl that one day she would become the mistress of a king. After this she became known by the nickname Reinette – which means 'little queen'.

In 1741, she married and became Madame d'Etoiles. Reinette met Louis XV at the masked Yew Tree Ball, and indeed soon became the king's mistress. She legally separated from her husband, and Louis XV made her Marquise de Pompadour. She died in April 1764.

TIME WINDOWS

Using the tremendous reserves of power on the damaged ship, the droids have opened windows to eighteenth-century France. They are trying to locate Reinette at the age of 37 (the age of the ship), but the windows are not accurate enough, so they open many of them, all along her lifeline. The relative time between the ship and France is not fixed: a few minutes may pass on the ship, but many months or even years have gone by in Reinette's world. So the Doctor appears not to age, but he sees Reinette at various points in her life.

COMPATIBILITY

Programmed to repair the ship in any way that they can, the droids use 'components' from the bodies of the crew and passengers as spare parts. A human eye replaces a damaged camera lens; a heart (see above) operates as an efficient fluid pump…

With the main memory circuits destroyed, the droids need to replace the computer command circuit. They assume that the brain of the real Madame de Pompadour, at the same age as the ship, can form a suitable alternative to the damaged systems.

SS MADAME DE POMPADOUR

Shown here are some of the original designs for the ship. While the interior was created as a studio set, the exterior was a computer-generated image (CGI).

Top: The initial design for the ship's interior.
Middle row: Designs for (left) a heart-pump, (middle) a human-eye camera, (right) restraint couches.
Bottom: The design for the exterior of the spaceship was based on a turning key, reflecting the roman-à-clef nature of Girl in the Fireplace.

SCRIPTING THE CLOCKWORK ROBOTS

The writer for this episode was Steven Moffat, who also wrote the 2005 **Doctor Who** stories *The Empty Child* and *The Doctor Dances* (see page 30). He describes the central character of this story – the girl in the fireplace:

'Reinette Poisson is a girl with one dream: to be the consort of a king. She has been trained, educated and refined into one of the most beautiful and learned women of her age. A dancer, an artist, an actress, a friend to philosophers and writers, and – one day, she hopes – the lover of Louis XV of France.

'But Reinette has nightmares, too. Some nights, she will hear the deep, slow tick of a clock – and, turning, see that the clock on the mantel is broken. She will feel that something is close to her in the shadows of her room. Under her bed. Outside her window. Just out of sight in the corridor behind her. Something that ticks, something more machine than human. Something that wants her.

'In her dream, sometimes she sees a strange metal world of clanging corridors and clicking chambers, where strange Tick Tock men in grinning masks mass in the shadows – and somehow she knows these clockwork creatures dream of her too.

'But, in the confusion of her nightmares, there is also hope. A man is coming. A man who saved her once in the past and will one day return to save her future ...

'At a magical fireside that is the gateway between one world and another, the girl with one dream will meet a man with two hearts. And she might just break them both.'

SCRIPT EXTRACT

In the light of a single candle, we can see so little. It is dressed in contemporary clothes, lace, ruffles –

– a shadow across its face. An impression of a contemporary wig.

The DOCTOR faces this creature across the bed.

STAGING THE BALL

Recreating the spectacular majesty of Versailles for television was a huge challenge for the **Doctor Who** production team – even without having to add alien Clockwork Robots. But it was a challenge that they rose to magnificently, as the pictures on these pages show.

Left: Reinette is ready for the ball.
Above: The Clockwork Man's mechanisms were operated by rods from behind.
Top: A mask gets some final attention.

A finished mask (left) and a mask at an earlier stage of design (right), before painting and texturing.

SCRIPT EXTRACT

The DOCTOR strides over to the trapped CLOCKWORK MAN, snatches off its wig and mask.

Revealed: a glass dome, crammed with a spinning, ticking marvel of clockwork. No trace of a face. Just cogs and spinning devices.

The DOCTOR stares, like he's awestruck.

MAKING THE CLOCKWORK ROBOT

Top: Rose meets a Clockwork Man.
Above: The Doctor confronts a Clockwork Robot at the ball.

Although only seen briefly in the finished episode, the Clockwork Robot was every bit as beautiful as the Doctor says. There was a single head and shoulders for the Clockwork Robot, which was dressed in a costume, wig and mask.

Neill Gorton and his team at Millennium FX worked from a design 'mood sheet' showing pictures of carriage clocks and close-ups of clockwork constructions. From this they designed and then built the Clockwork Robot's head and shoulders, and also the arm.

Constructed by Millennium FX, the head was tilted and swivelled by means of levers inside the chest and operated from behind. The clockwork inside the head actually worked – the various wheels and cogs form an intricate, working mechanism. The arm was also fully functional. With its various attachment tools, it was operated using a system of flywheels and wires.

The result was a beautifully intricate and totally convincing clockwork robot.

Left: The Clockwork Woman is revealed.
Above: Neill Gorton of Millennium FX
with a clockwork friend.

THE CYBERMEN

THE CYBERMEN

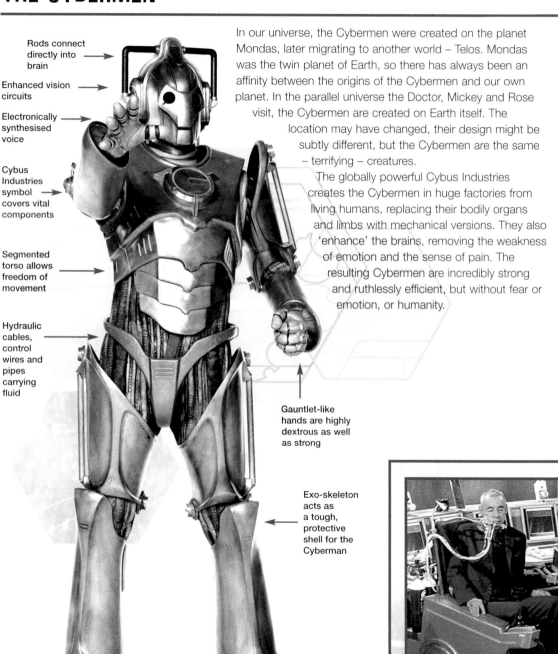

Rods connect directly into brain →

Enhanced vision circuits →

Electronically synthesised voice →

Cybus Industries symbol covers vital components →

Segmented torso allows freedom of movement →

Hydraulic cables, control wires and pipes carrying fluid →

In our universe, the Cybermen were created on the planet Mondas, later migrating to another world – Telos. Mondas was the twin planet of Earth, so there has always been an affinity between the origins of the Cybermen and our own planet. In the parallel universe the Doctor, Mickey and Rose visit, the Cybermen are created on Earth itself. The location may have changed, their design might be subtly different, but the Cybermen are the same – terrifying – creatures.

The globally powerful Cybus Industries creates the Cybermen in huge factories from living humans, replacing their bodily organs and limbs with mechanical versions. They also 'enhance' the brains, removing the weakness of emotion and the sense of pain. The resulting Cybermen are incredibly strong and ruthlessly efficient, but without fear or emotion, or humanity.

Gauntlet-like hands are highly dextrous as well as strong

Exo-skeleton acts as a tough, protective shell for the Cyberman

THE CYBER CONTROLLER

The leader of the Cybermen is the Cyber Controller. On the parallel Earth where the Doctor and his friends witness the birth of the Cybermen, the Controller is the Cybermen's creator, John Lumic, converted into a Cyberman. The Cyber Controller has the same basic design as the Cybermen, but differs in several ways.

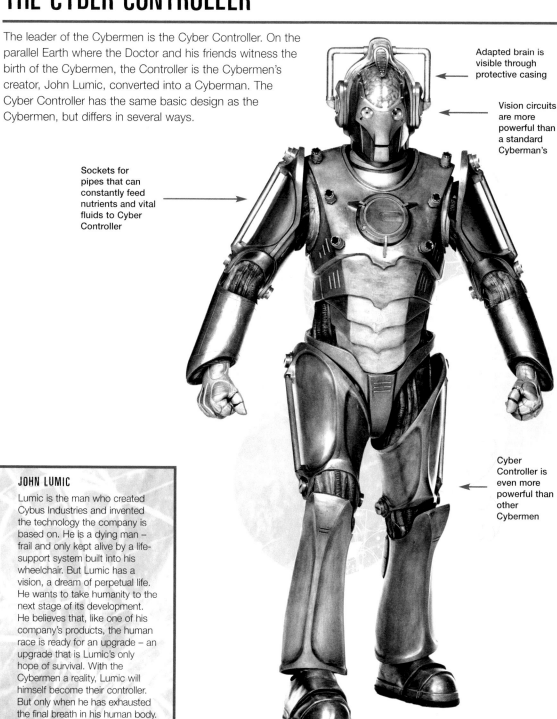

Adapted brain is visible through protective casing

Vision circuits are more powerful than a standard Cyberman's

Sockets for pipes that can constantly feed nutrients and vital fluids to Cyber Controller

Cyber Controller is even more powerful than other Cybermen

JOHN LUMIC

Lumic is the man who created Cybus Industries and invented the technology the company is based on. He is a dying man – frail and only kept alive by a life-support system built into his wheelchair. But Lumic has a vision, a dream of perpetual life. He wants to take humanity to the next stage of its development. He believes that, like one of his company's products, the human race is ready for an upgrade – an upgrade that is Lumic's only hope of survival. With the Cybermen a reality, Lumic will himself become their controller. But only when he has exhausted the final breath in his human body.

THE CYBERMEN

RISE OF THE CYBERMEN and THE AGE OF STEEL

Written by
Tom MacRae
Featuring
the Tenth Doctor,
Rose and Mickey
First broadcast
spring 2006
2 episodes

The Doctor, Rose and Mickey arrive on Earth. Or do they? There are differences that tell them they have arrived on a parallel world. Huge Zeppelins hang in the sky over London. Rose's father is alive – a rich and powerful man – but Rose herself has never been born. And information is controlled and disseminated by the powerful Cybus Industries.

John Lumic, the owner and director of Cybus, has plans to take his corporation's control even further – beyond information and technology. As people disappear off the streets and Mickey meets an alternative version of himself, can the Doctor and his friends stop the creation of one of the Doctor's most deadly and fearsome foes?

CYBUS INDUSTRIES

Cybus Industries has advanced the development of the whole planet with its inventions and products. Owned and run by the charismatic John Lumic, Cybus disseminates all news and current affairs information via a daily download sent directly to the earpods of every subscriber. But now Lumic wants to go further. Crippled and confined to a wheelchair, he believes his only hope of survival is another upgrade – this time to humanity itself. He sees the human brain as the most complex piece of software in existence, and plans to take it forward to the next stage. Cybus can improve the brain – removing painful and inefficient emotions. Cybus can upgrade the body – replacing inefficient organs and limbs with durable, strong plastic and steel.

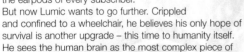

Left: The Cybermen crash the party.
Opposite (top): The Cybermen take over.
Opposite (bottom right): A Cyberman on
the Cybus Industries zeppelin.

SCRIPTING THE CYBERMEN

Above: The Cyber Controller declares
the Age of Steel.
Right: Special guest – the President.

SCRIPT EXTRACT

ROSE
But what are they?

THE DOCTOR
Cybermen

SMASH! - the French windows
shatter -

SMASH! - another set -

SMASH! - another set -
glass flying

THE CYBERMEN enter the
room. Tall, steel giants.
Impassive metal faces.
Hints of Art Deco in their
design. Cyberman after
Cyberman after Cyberman.

The job of reviving the Cybermen and updating them for the new series was given to writer Tom MacRae. MacRae has written for various television series and has also scripted several one-off plays. He remembered the Cybermen from the original series as 'big silver robot people', and felt that in their later stories they had degenerated into mere monsters that looked impressive but had little credible motivation or purpose. This was something he was determined to put right with his own scripts. He explains:

'The new versions look wonderful too, of course. But I wanted more than just spectacle. I wanted to give the Cybermen a proper place in the scheme of things – a motivation and a plan. I think, given their back-story, the Cybermen are very interesting and I wanted to draw that out. I wanted to get away from the straightforward monstrous villains of the end of the original series and make them more *human*, and therefore more scary.

'My starting point, and it's true to the original idea behind the Cybermen when they first appeared, is what if science went wrong? What if medical augmentation went too far? I wanted to approach that in a more modern way.

'The story itself is actually a very simple and very sad human story. It's a downfall story that's become almost supernatural, though there's no magic, it's all science. Lumic is not an evil genius, he's a man who is very ill and desperate to save himself, and in the process he's gone a bit mad. But everything he does and everything that happens stems from that.

'A good script needs a mix of both story and set pieces. I don't like horror stories that are all set piece with no narrative to bind them. The set pieces have to be there for a reason, and a reason which we understand. So when the Cybermen crash through the windows it's an impressive and exciting sequence, but we know *why* they're doing it.'

THE CYBERMEN

CREATING THE CYBERMEN

The design of the new Cybermen was a month-long process, involving every part of the **Doctor Who** design team. Eventually, with a rough design agreed and the Art Deco style of the story settled on, the job of finalising that design and creating the Cybermen themselves fell to Millennium FX.

First they designed the head, which had to move independently of the body, rather than being a 'helmet' with restricted movement, as had been the case with previous Cyber costumes.

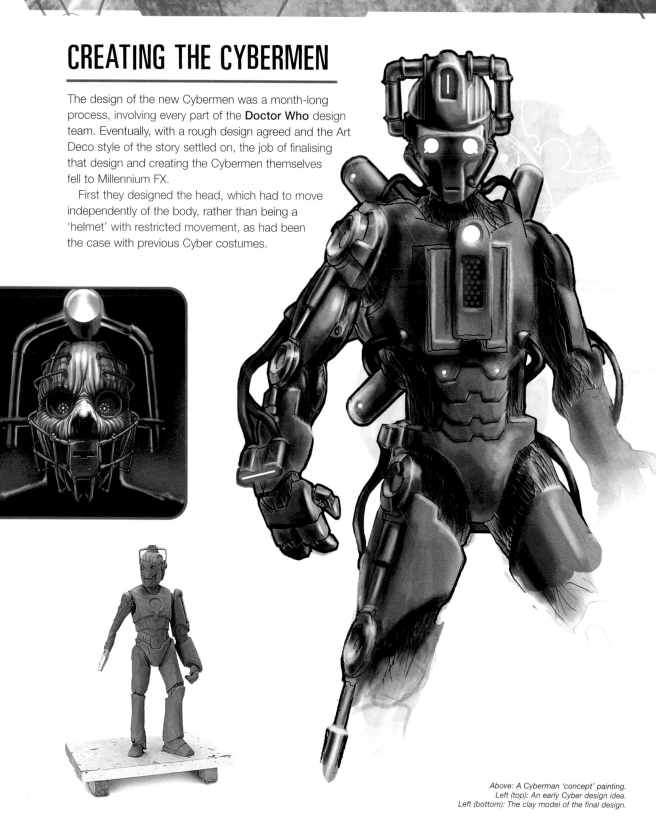

Above: A Cyberman 'concept' painting.
Left (top): An early Cyber design idea.
Left (bottom): The clay model of the final design.

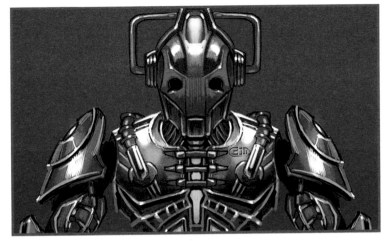

*The pictures on this page show early ideas and digital concept paintings from the **Doctor Who** design department and (bottom right) Millennium FX.*

BUILDING THE CYBERMEN

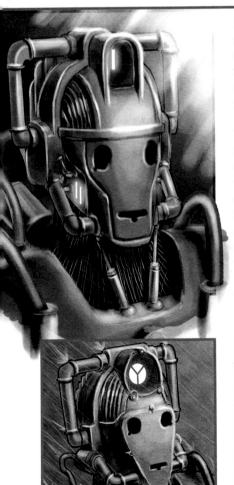

Millennium FX created various drawings and clay models of possible Cyber heads before making a maquette – a small model – of the final design from clay. Next they made a full-sized clay sculpture of the entire Cyberman and took moulds from it to create the various parts of the costume from fibreglass.

Ten Cyberman costumes were made. The head was in nine sections, while the rest of the body had over 40 component pieces. They achieved the metallic effect by adding aluminium powder to the final layer of fibreglass, and hand-polishing each separate piece until it gleamed. The exception to this was the hands – which were gloves made from soft, silver-tinted silicon. The result was the most terrifying Cyberman design yet.

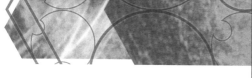

Right: The Cyber Controller as he appeared in Attack of the Cybermen. *Bottom left: An early sketch of the Controller's head. Bottom right: The Controller emerges.*

REVIVING THE CYBER CONTROLLER

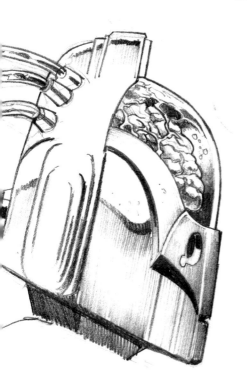

The Cybermen have been led by their Cyber Controller in two previous **Doctor Who** stories – *The Tomb of the Cybermen* and *Attack of the Cybermen*.

In *The Tomb of the Cybermen*, first broadcast 2–23 September 1967, the second incarnation of the Doctor managed to seal the Cybermen back into their ice tombs on the planet Telos. In *Attack of the Cybermen*, first broadcast 5–12 January 1985, the Sixth Doctor battled against a revived and redesigned Cyber Controller.

The Cyber Controller for the new 2006 series of **Doctor Who** was again a Cyberman of a slightly different design. This Controller was also, for a while, wired into a Cyber throne.

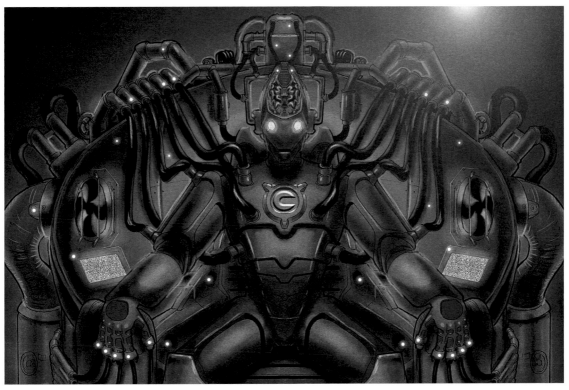

Top: A design painting of the Controller on his throne.
Above: The Controller as he actually appeared.
Right: The design for Lumic's wheelchair.

THE DÆMONS

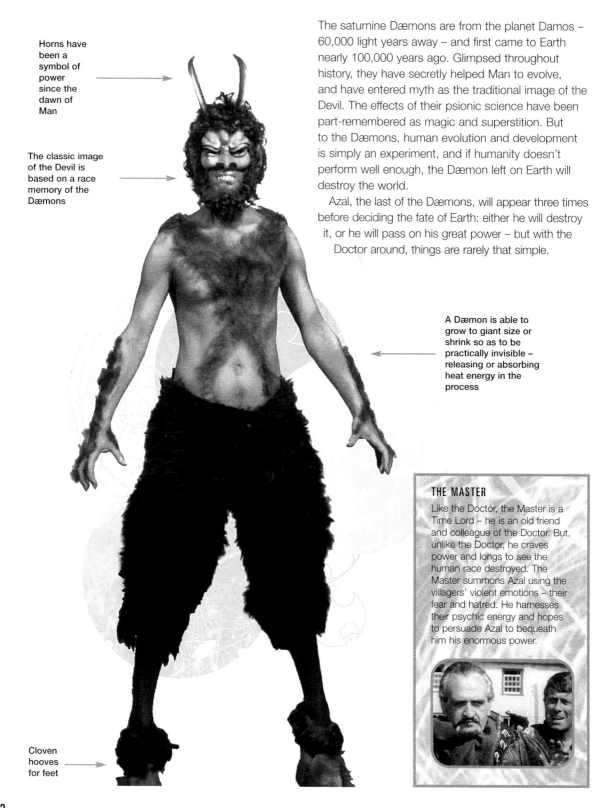

Horns have been a symbol of power since the dawn of Man

The classic image of the Devil is based on a race memory of the Dæmons

The saturnine Dæmons are from the planet Damos – 60,000 light years away – and first came to Earth nearly 100,000 years ago. Glimpsed throughout history, they have secretly helped Man to evolve, and have entered myth as the traditional image of the Devil. The effects of their psionic science have been part-remembered as magic and superstition. But to the Dæmons, human evolution and development is simply an experiment, and if humanity doesn't perform well enough, the Dæmon left on Earth will destroy the world.

Azal, the last of the Dæmons, will appear three times before deciding the fate of Earth: either he will destroy it, or he will pass on his great power – but with the Doctor around, things are rarely that simple.

A Dæmon is able to grow to giant size or shrink so as to be practically invisible – releasing or absorbing heat energy in the process

THE MASTER

Like the Doctor, the Master is a Time Lord – he is an old friend and colleague of the Doctor. But, unlike the Doctor, he craves power and longs to see the human race destroyed. The Master summons Azal using the villagers' violent emotions – their fear and hatred. He harnesses their psychic energy and hopes to persuade Azal to bequeath him his enormous power.

Cloven hooves for feet

The Doctor is captured by sinister morris dancers working for the Master.

THE DÆMONS

The Doctor and Jo visit Devil's End, where Professor Horner is excavating an ancient burial mound. But inside is the crashed spaceship of Azal, last of the Dæmons, an ancient race who've been experimenting with human evolution. The Dæmon has been summoned by the Master, who is posing as the local vicar and manipulating the local villagers.

With the Brigadier and UNIT unable to reach them, the Doctor and Jo enlist the help of a local white witch to combat the revived Dæmon, an animated gargoyle, hostile villagers and some homicidal morris dancers.

Azal appears for a final time and prepares to kill the Doctor, but Jo's offer to die in the Doctor's place confounds Azal, and Azal is destroyed.

Written by
Guy Leopold
Featuring
the Third Doctor,
UNIT and Jo
First broadcast
22 May 1971 –
19 June 1971
5 episodes

DEVIL'S END

The whole area is steeped in the Dæmons' mythology and black magic. Nearby villages include Witchwood and Satanhill, while the village pub is called The Cloven Hoof. The burial mound containing Azal's ship is called the Devil's Hump and local legends predict death and destruction if it is opened… Previous attempts to excavate the Hump have ended in disaster.

In the notorious cavern beneath the church, the witches of the seventeenth century hid from the fires of witch-hunter Matthew Hopkins.

THE HEAT BARRIER

Using the psionic science of the Dæmons and the power of the black magic coven he commands, the Master creates a heat barrier around Devil's End to keep UNIT out, trapping the Doctor and Jo in the village. The barrier is a huge dome, a mile high at the centre, above the village church. The barrier can be seen only as a 'heat haze' and a charred line across the ground.

The Doctor is able to help UNIT create an energy exchanger to make a hole in the barrier, so the Brigadier and his troops can enter.

BOK

Bok is the pet name given by the Master to a stone gargoyle-like figure animated by the power of Azal. The gargoyle's eyes glow red and it can fire a destructive force from its finger. The Doctor escapes from Bok by warding it off with a trowel – iron has ancient magical properties – and chanting an incantation (part of a Venusian lullaby: 'Close your eyes, my darling – well, three of them, at least…').

Bok explodes when shot, but reforms and attacks the UNIT troops again. When Azal is destroyed, Bok becomes inanimate stone.

THE DALEK EMPEROR

The supreme leader of the Daleks – their Emperor – has taken several different forms in the past. After the Great Time War wiped out most of the Dalek race, the few survivors were ruled by an Emperor who, having led them from the wilderness and created new Dalek life, believed itself to be the god of all Daleks.

This enormous Dalek Emperor is wired into the Daleks' flagship. The surviving Daleks have waited, slowly infiltrating humanity and taking the refugees and dispossessed to create new Daleks, only one cell in a billion being 'pure' enough for them to use. Now, with an army of new Daleks, the Emperor is ready to purify the Earth – by fire.

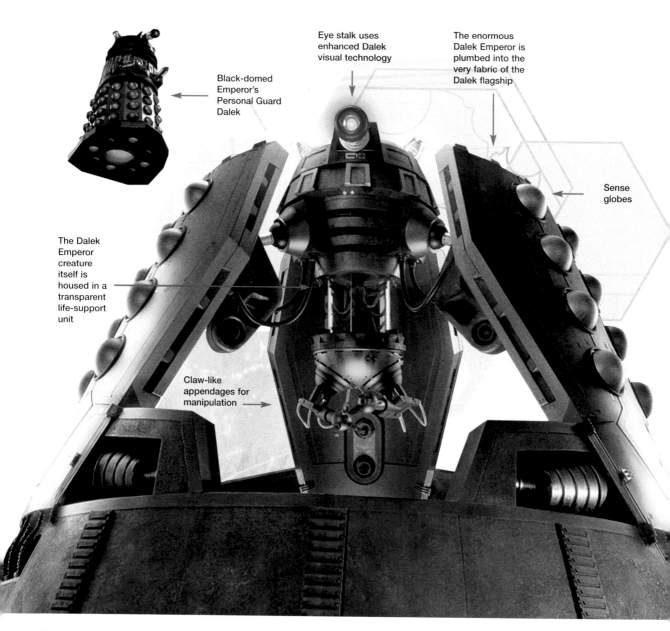

Eye stalk uses enhanced Dalek visual technology

The enormous Dalek Emperor is plumbed into the very fabric of the Dalek flagship

Black-domed Emperor's Personal Guard Dalek

Sense globes

The Dalek Emperor creature itself is housed in a transparent life-support unit

Claw-like appendages for manipulation

The Doctor meets the other survivors of the Great Time War.

BAD WOLF and THE PARTING OF THE WAYS

The Doctor, Rose and Jack find themselves teleported to the Game Station, where they are forced to take part in deadly television shows. But an even more deadly menace is approaching – a fleet of Dalek ships poised to invade Earth. Rescuing Rose from the Dalek flagship, the Doctor and Jack meet the Dalek Emperor – now convinced it is the god of the Daleks and about to purify the Earth by fire.

Captain Jack organises the defence of the station, while the Doctor returns Rose to Earth and works to create a Delta Wave that will destroy the Daleks. As the Daleks kill Jack and corner the Doctor, it is Rose who returns to save the day. But her solution will cost the Doctor his own life.

Written by
Russell T Davies
Featuring
the Ninth Doctor, Rose and Captain Jack
First broadcast
11 June 2005 –
18 June 2005
2 episodes

THE GAME STATION

The Game Station is Satellite Five (from *The Long Game*, see page 41) 100 years on. Run by the Bad Wolf Corporation, it broadcasts game shows and reality TV to the population of Earth. The entire output goes through the brain of the Controller – a woman who was installed into the station's systems as a child. In fact, she is the conduit through which the Daleks are running the Game Station. She is able to bring the Doctor to the station and warn him about the Daleks. Realising her betrayal, the Daleks exterminate her.

THE TIME WAR

Records of the Great Time War are scarce and unreliable, but after the Time Lords sought to eliminate the Daleks by sending the Doctor back in time to prevent their creation, the Daleks began to retaliate. As negotiations broke down, a full-scale war erupted within the Time Vortex and beyond that in the Ultimate Void. The Time Lords reached back into history for ever-more-terrible weapons, while the Daleks unleashed the Deathsmiths of Goth... For centuries the war raged, unseen by most of the universe. But the Higher Species watched and wept...

THE BAD WOLF

Throughout her time with the Ninth Doctor, Rose is aware of references to the 'Bad Wolf', though she has no idea what they mean. Then she finds the Game Station is run by the Bad Wolf Corporation. Returned, unwillingly, to Earth, Rose realises the references are a message telling her she can save the Doctor and humanity. Spurred on by this, she opens the very heart of the TARDIS and becomes possessed by the power of the Vortex itself. She uses it to defeat the Daleks, and to send the Bad Wolf messages back into her past.

THE DALEK EMPEROR

Right: The Dalek Emperor in The Parting of the Ways.
Bottom left: Davros is inside the Emperor in Remembrance of the Daleks.
Bottom right: The Dalek Emperor in comic-strip form.

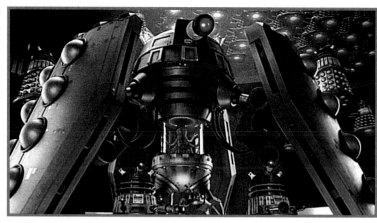

EMPERORS OF THE DALEKS

The Dalek Emperor has taken several forms over the long history of the Daleks. According to some records, the first Dalek Emperor had a casing built from Flidor gold, quartz and the sap of the Arkellis flower that grew on Skaro before the Thousand Year War that led to the creation of the Daleks. It had an enlarged dome section.

Many years later, during a time of strife between two Dalek factions, the Imperial Daleks were led by an Emperor that was their creator, Davros, housed inside a standard Dalek casing, but again with an enlarged dome.

More impressive was the enormous Dalek Emperor that ruled the Dalek race from their huge underground city on Skaro. Plumbed into the very structure of the Dalek City, the Emperor was badly damaged – possibly even destroyed – in the Great Civil War caused by the Doctor introducing the so-called Human Factor into the Dalek race. This caused infected Daleks to question the authority of the Emperor – and indeed the whole Dalek creed.

Order was eventually restored and the renegade Daleks destroyed. The Emperor led the Daleks into the Great Time War against the Time Lords that resulted in the apparent destruction of both races. The leader that survived and rebuilt the Dalek race, using genetic cellular material from kidnapped humans, saw itself as god of all Daleks.

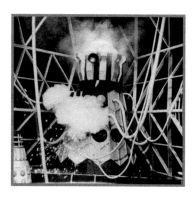

Left: The Emperor's throne room in The Evil of the Daleks.
Below: Civil war among the Daleks.

Bottom left: The Emperor's personal guards defend him.
Bottom right: The Emperor's guard with additional weaponry.

THE EMPEROR'S PERSONAL GUARDS

Traditionally, the Dalek Emperor's personal guards are distinguished from other Daleks by their black dome sections. On the Dalek flagship they hover close to the Emperor, constantly observing and protecting their leader. These Daleks also have an additional, highly powerful weapon in place of the sucker arm that ordinary Daleks use.

On Skaro, before the Great Civil War, the Black Dalek Leaders formed the personal guard of the Dalek Emperor, which was built into the very fabric of the Dalek City. During the Civil War they fought to protect the Emperor from rogue Daleks that the Doctor had impregnated with the Human Factor and that questioned the authority of the Emperor. Despite the Emperor's attempts to prevent the battle spreading into the Throne

Room, its personal guards were forced to retreat and the Emperor was severely damaged. The Doctor described the Civil War as 'The final end'.

The Dalek Supreme – one of the High Council of Daleks – has also been distinguished by its black livery. It was seen during the attempted Dalek invasion of Earth.

27

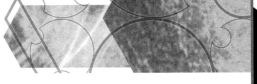

Right: The design for the Emperor.
Bottom left: Miniature effects designer Mike Tucker at work.
Bottom right: The completed model of the Emperor.

DEVISING THE EMPEROR

Shown here are the original designs for the Dalek Emperor on the Dalek flagship, and pictures of the Emperor being built. The Emperor itself was designed by Dan Walker, and was built by the **Doctor Who** miniatures team, led by Mike Tucker. The Dalek creature was designed and built by Neill Gorton of Millennium FX.

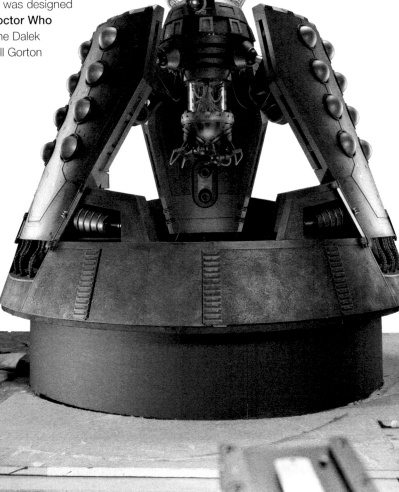

SCRIPT EXTRACT

… A huge, hundred-foot metal thing of beauty; more complicated, but based on a Dalek design. Pipes and tubes spreading out to the ship. At the centre – not the very top – a glass bowl, in which something blue twitches, suspended in swirling fluids.

The Emperor has a Dalek-like grate to its voice, but it's much more subtle. It's not Davros, but it's as eloquent. And all around the Emperor, gantries and walkways. Going way up high; and way down low… FX DALEKS moving about on all levels.

Above: An early concept painting of the Emperor. Left: The team responsible for the model Emperor: (back, from left) Nick Kool, Alan Brannan, Mike Tucker, Alan 'Spike' Graham, Liz Trott; (front, from left) Dave Houghton and Peter Tyler.

THE EMPTY CHILD

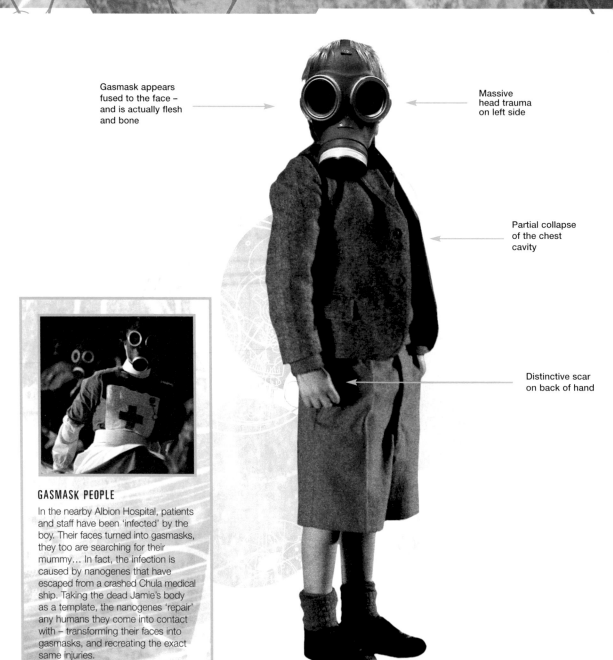

Gasmask appears fused to the face – and is actually flesh and bone

Massive head trauma on left side

Partial collapse of the chest cavity

Distinctive scar on back of hand

GASMASK PEOPLE

In the nearby Albion Hospital, patients and staff have been 'infected' by the boy. Their faces turned into gasmasks, they too are searching for their mummy… In fact, the infection is caused by nanogenes that have escaped from a crashed Chula medical ship. Taking the dead Jamie's body as a template, the nanogenes 'repair' any humans they come into contact with – transforming their faces into gasmasks, and recreating the exact same injuries.

In the war-torn Britain of 1941, a young girl – Nancy – is living on the blitzed streets of London. To survive, she and other street children steal food from the houses of people sheltering from German air raids. The children regard Nancy as their leader. But they are haunted by another child – a small boy wearing a gasmask, constantly searching for his mother.

The child can project his voice – incessantly asking 'Are you my mummy?' – through any communications equipment: the (unconnected) TARDIS telephone, a radio, even a music box and a typewriter. The Empty Child is actually Nancy's 'brother' Jamie. He was killed in an air raid, and has been brought to life by alien technology.

The Doctor tries to solve the mystery of the Empty Child.

THE EMPTY CHILD and THE DOCTOR DANCES

Looking for a crashed spaceship in London, the Doctor and Rose arrive during the Blitz of 1941 and discover that people have been infected by a strange, 'empty' child. The crashed ship was a Chula medical ship, and the interior was filled with nanogenes, which were released in the crash. These microscopic devices are programmed to repair Chula Warriors on the battlefield. Now the nanogenes are set to remodel the entire human race on a terrified child augmented with fearsome military powers.

With the help of Captain Jack Harkness, and armed only with a sonic screwdriver and a banana, the Doctor and Rose reunite Jamie with his mother, and the nanogenes recognise – and reverse – the damage.

Written by
Steven Moffat
Featuring
the Ninth Doctor, Rose and Captain Jack
First broadcast
21 May 2005 –
28 May 2005
2 episodes

NANOGENES

The nanogenes do not understand the human physiology. They use the first human they find – Jamie – as a template and 'repair' all the others they come into contact with through him.

First the doctors and nurses who treat the child are affected, then the patients those doctors and nurses treat, and so on. The infected people have no life signs – but they do not die. They have also been augmented and are ready to defend the crashed ship, and the Empty Child, with tremendous alien power at their disposal.

THE CHULA SHIP

The Chula Ship – a large mauve cylinder – fell on Limehouse Green Station and is now cordoned off and under guard.

Captain Jack claims it is the last surviving fully equipped Chula Warship. But in fact he is lying, so as to be able to sell the ship to the Time Agency – it is actually an ambulance, which he steered close to the TARDIS as bait for the Doctor and Rose (whom he believes to be Time Agents). Jack has parked the ship where he knows a German bomb will destroy it – after he gets his money, but before the Agents realise he has lied.

NANCY AND THE CHILDREN

Nancy looks after the children who live rough on the streets of London during the Blitz. She organises the theft of food from houses during air raids. She enjoys mothering the children, making sure they behave in each house like guests rather than thieves.

The Doctor realises that Nancy has lost someone close to her – Jamie – and is looking after the children as a way of making up for it. He also realises that she is not Jamie's sister, but his mother – the mummy the Empty Child is desperately trying to find.

THE EMPTY CHILD

BEHIND THE MASKS

While they looked completely authentic, the gasmasks used in making *The Empty Child* and *The Doctor Dances* were actually created specially for the episodes by Millennium FX. The eye pieces were indeed taken from real gasmasks – but modern, Russian ones. The designers sculpted the rest of the mask in clay and then took a mould of this model, from which the actual masks were made. Next they fitted the eye pieces and backed them with dark material to obscure the actors' eyes. The protruding filter was also specially moulded, with a section of it actually made from a baked-bean tin!

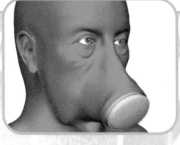

The sequence in which Doctor Constantine turns into one of the Gasmask People was created by The Mill using computer-generated images (CGI). It was one of the most unsettling effects produced for the series. In fact, the story was packed with memorable images, with one sequence winning a viewers' award.

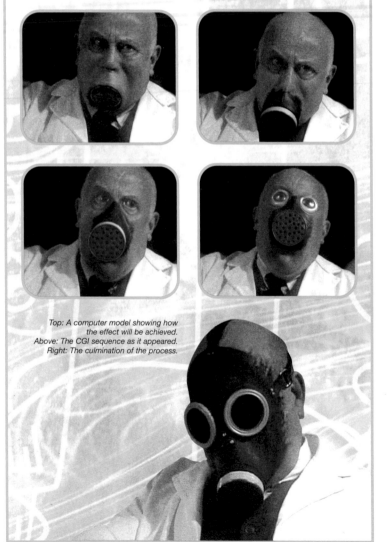

Top: A computer model showing how the effect will be achieved.
Above: The CGI sequence as it appeared.
Right: The culmination of the process.

Above and right (top): Impressive effects shots of London in the Blitz.
Far right (top): Rose hanging from a (model) barrage balloon.
Right: Actress Billie Piper falling against a green background.
Far right: The final effect, with the green background replaced.

Billie Piper is hung from wires to simulate her fall.

RECREATING THE BLITZ

One of the greatest challenges in making *The Empty Child* and *The Doctor Dances* was to recreate the London of 1941 – and, in particular, an air raid. But, not only did the production team, led by director James Hawes, need to create an air raid, they also had to put Rose right in the middle of it.

This was achieved by combining live-action footage of Billie Piper playing Rose, with CGI of the attacking planes and the London landscape, and a miniature barrage balloon created and filmed by the model unit.

THE GELTH

The Gelth are ectoplasmic, ethereal, wraith-like creatures, which possess the dead at the Cardiff undertakers Sneed and Company, in the late nineteenth century. They are trans-dimensional aliens that can travel through the junction point between two worlds, using beings with psychic ability as a bridge between dimensions.

Essentially gaseous creatures, in this world the Gelth 'live' in the gas pipes – the environment most suited to them. They claim there are very few Gelth left; they are the last of their kind and are facing extinction. But in fact they plan to invade the planet in their billions, killing humans and then possessing the bodies of the dead.

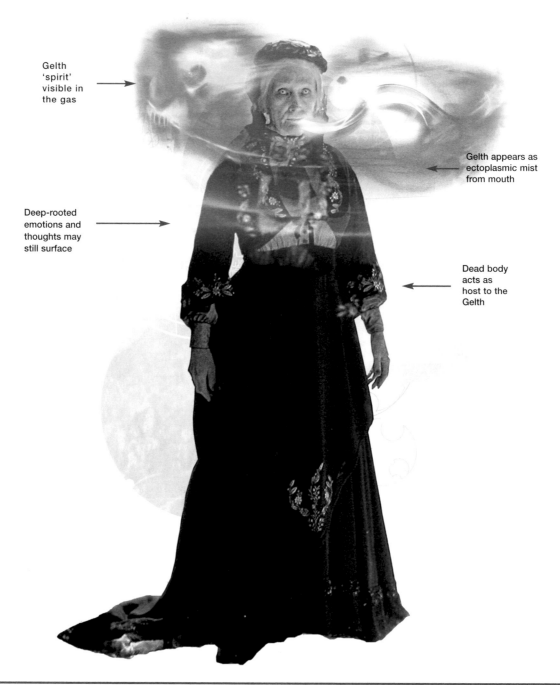

Gelth 'spirit' visible in the gas

Gelth appears as ectoplasmic mist from mouth

Deep-rooted emotions and thoughts may still surface

Dead body acts as host to the Gelth

The Doctor and Rose are trapped with the Gelth in the cellar.

THE UNQUIET DEAD

The Doctor and Rose arrive in Cardiff on Christmas Eve in 1869. The Doctor meets Charles Dickens, while Rose finds herself at Gabriel Sneed's funeral parlour, where the dead are getting far too lively.

Enlisting the help of Dickens, Sneed and Gwyneth, the Doctor and Rose discover that the dead are being possessed by an alien race, the Gelth. Gwyneth is psychic and is able to contact them through a séance. They claim they are looking for new bodies so their race can survive.

Gwyneth creates a gateway for the Gelth to enter the real world. But they reveal that their true intentions are to kill everyone and live in their bodies. Gwyneth sacrifices herself to close the gateway and leave the Gelth stranded.

Written by
Mark Gatiss
Featuring
the Ninth Doctor
and Rose
First broadcast
9 April 2005
1 episode

GWYNETH

Sneed's servant girl, Gwyneth, came to work for him after her parents died of influenza when she was 12 years old. She is gifted with second sight and is able to track down Mrs Peace when the Gelth possess the old woman's dead body.

Gwyneth considers the Gelth to be angels, sent by her dead mother. But after they arrive and reveal their true nature, the Doctor is able to convince her of the Gelth's evil intentions. Although her body is already dead, enough of Gwyneth lives on to destroy the Gelth by igniting the gas in Sneed's morgue.

CHARLES DICKENS

Charles Dickens is in the last year of his life when he meets the Doctor and Rose. He is a tired, sceptical old man and is at first wary of the Doctor, accusing him of staging the phantasmagoric intrusion at the theatre. But the Doctor soon wins Dickens over by telling him he is Dickens' number-one fan.

At first Dickens does not believe in the existence of the Gelth, but their manifestation during Gwyneth's séance soon convinces him. He is shocked and disappointed to think that all his life he has misunderstood the true nature of the world. But by the end of the story, he is ready to open his mind to new ideas and to broaden his outlook.

THE GELTH

Right: Mrs Peace is possessed.
Below: Mrs Peace and her grandson,
Redpath, under Gelth control.

ZOMBIES

Many of the bodies brought to Sneed's funeral parlour just won't stay dead – in fact they're up and about, and off to the theatre. Sneed claims that one deceased sexton almost walked in on his own memorial service, and the late Mrs Peace kills her grandson, Redpath, and goes on to attend Charles Dickens' reading, as she had planned before her death.

In truth, the bodies are possessed by the Gelth, which emerge from the gas pipes as screeching blue ectoplasm, and enter the corpses, bringing them back to unnatural life.

But the 'union' of Gelth and body is weak and after a short while the zombie collapses, once more a lifeless corpse, as the Gelth leaves it.

OUT OF THIN AIR

While the walking dead at Sneed and Company were actors made up to look like cadavers, the Gelth themselves were computer-generated images (CGI), created using the face of actress Zoe Thorne as a starting point for the design of the creatures.

Above left: The Gelth appear.
Left: Behind the scenes at the séance.
Above: Gwyneth summons the spirits.

WHERE THE DICKENS?!

To create Victorian Cardiff, the **Doctor Who** team actually went to Swansea, which offered a more authentic-looking Victorian setting. The transformation of present-day Swansea into Cardiff on Christmas Eve, 1869 was a huge undertaking. Cars had to be excluded from the area, street signs replaced, extras dressed in appropriate clothing and made up with Victorian hairstyles. And snow had to be created. This attention to the smallest detail helped create a totally convincing Victorian winter scene.

Above left: The Doctor and Rose in 'Cardiff'.
Left: Careful attention is paid to the background details.
Above: The TARDIS arrives in Victorian Wales.

MAGNUS GREEL

The infamous minister of justice Magnus Greel was nicknamed the Butcher of Brisbane. He sent 100,000 people to their deaths and was branded a war criminal after the fall of the Icelandic Alliance. He escaped in his experimental time cabinet, arriving in nineteenth-century China. He assumed the identity of the Chinese god Weng-Chiang, and was helped by members of the Tong of the Black Scorpion.

Greel's time cabinet is powered by dangerous zygma energy, and the journey distorted his appearance. Dying, Greel tries to augment his life force by draining the energy from young women, with a distillation device. Defeated by the Doctor, and desperate for nutrition, Greel dies from cellular collapse when the Doctor pushes him into the distillation chamber.

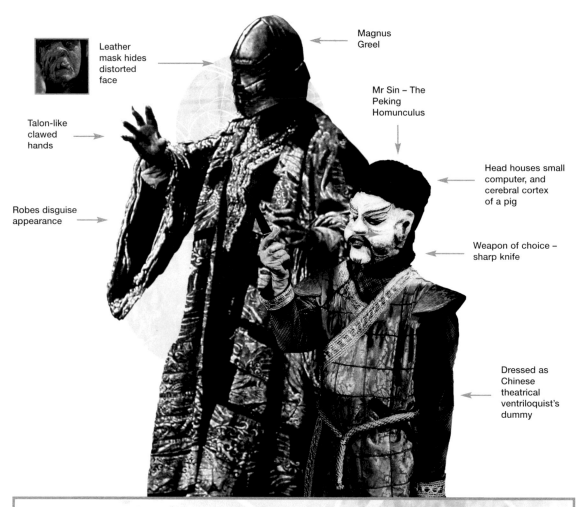

Leather mask hides distorted face

Magnus Greel

Mr Sin – The Peking Homunculus

Talon-like clawed hands

Head houses small computer, and cerebral cortex of a pig

Robes disguise appearance

Weapon of choice – sharp knife

Dressed as Chinese theatrical ventriloquist's dummy

MR SIN – THE PEKING HOMUNCULUS

Greel has brought the Peking Homunculus back through time, disguising it as Li H'Sen Chang's ventriloquist's dummy – Mr Sin. The Homunculus was made as a toy for the children of the commissioner of the Icelandic Alliance in the year 5000. It contained a series of magnetic fields operating on a printed circuit and a small computer as well as one organic component – the cerebral cortex of a pig. But the pig's brain took over the Homunculus, and the swinish instinct became dominant – it hated humanity and revelled in carnage. Eventually it is this instinctive nature that drives it to rebel against Greel.

Actor Deep Roy (pictured here on the right) played Mr Sin in some scenes, while a dummy was used in others.

THE TALONS OF WENG-CHIANG

The Doctor takes Leela to Victorian London to visit the music hall, but they witness a murder and are attacked by Chinese thugs from the Tong of the Black Scorpion. Faced with a giant rat hiding in the sewers, and a sinister stage-magician with an animated and homicidal ventriloquist's dummy, the Doctor loses all hope of a quiet evening out – he is facing Magnus Greel, a war criminal from the far future.

Greel has lost his time cabinet, and traced it to London. When he recovers it, the Doctor obtains the key, leading to a stand-off. Greel threatens the Doctor with a dragon statue that fires laser beams from its eyes. But the Doctor and his friends triumph, and Greel is killed.

Written by
Robert Holmes
Featuring
the Fourth Doctor
and Leela
First broadcast
26 February 1977 –
2 April 1977
6 episodes

LI H'SEN CHANG

The son of a peasant, Li H'Sen Chang's status has improved since he witnessed the arrival of Greel in his 'cabinet of light' and greeted him as the god Weng-Chiang. Now Chang tours the world helping Greel look for his missing time cabinet, which was taken by the emperor's soldiers and given to an Englishman.

Chang is now a magician, helped by the hypnotic powers that Greel has given him, and by his ventriloquist's dummy – Mr Sin. Betrayed by Greel, Chang is killed after his leg is bitten off by one of Greel's giant rats.

GIANT RATS

Greel's testing of the zygma beam has created enlarged animals as a side effect. The Doctor finds a huge money spider in the basement of the Palace Theatre. Greel uses the giant rats he has produced to guard the entrance through the sewers to his hidden base below the theatre.

The Doctor manages to rescue Leela from one of the rats by shooting it (with a Chinese firing piece that was – luckily – made in Birmingham). Another of the rats carries off Li H'Sen Chang, who later dies of his wounds.

LITEFOOT AND JAGO

Throughout this story, the Doctor and Leela are helped by Henry Gordon Jago (owner–manager of the Palace Theatre), and pathologist Professor George Litefoot. Jago's bluster and bluff manner cover a soft-hearted nature and he admits to Litefoot that 'I'm not so bally brave when it comes to it.'

Litefoot's father was palace attaché in China, and here he acquired Greel's time cabinet. He meets the Doctor and Leela while performing a post mortem for the police. Litefoot and Jago help the Doctor and Leela to defeat Greel.

THE JAGRAFESS

Heavily sunken eyes

Jagrafess needs to keep cool

Sharp-toothed mouth extruded from bodily mass

The Jagrafess lifespan is about 3000 years

Unearthly screeching is the only sound the Jagrafess makes

Viscous bodily fluids drip from mouth

Like its name, the Mighty Jagrafess of the Holy Hadrojassic Maxarodenfoe is huge. It exists, stretched out across the ceiling and roof of the control room, on Floor 500 of Satellite Five.

It is a vast expanse of flesh, with a sharp-toothed mouth, which communicates with the Editor through his earpiece. Since Satellite Five went online, 91 years before the events of *The Long Game*, the Jagrafess has shaped Mankind's development using the satellite's news reports.

By manipulating the news, the Jagrafess is able to develop a climate of fear. It can create an enemy that does not exist, or even use subliminal messaging to affect the economy or change a vote. It is playing a long game, controlling events for its own profit.

BEHIND THE SCENES

The enigmatic Editor (left) seems to be in charge of Satellite Five, though in fact he answers to the Jagrafess. But even the Jagrafess is not the real power behind the manipulation of the satellite's news reports. It has itself been installed by another, even more deadly and dangerous power to see that humanity follows a set pattern of events. As the Doctor and Rose later discover, the last Dalek survivors of the Time War are actually behind the manipulation of Mankind.

The Editor questions Rose and the Doctor as the Mighty Jagrafess looks down.

THE LONG GAME

Arriving on news-broadcasting station Satellite Five, the Doctor, Rose and their new companion Adam discover that broadcasting is not quite what they expected. Journalists channel information through chips embedded in their heads – and Adam soon gets himself a forehead upgrade. The journalists all hope to get promoted to Floor 500, where the Doctor and Rose find that the apparently all-powerful Editor actually works for an alien – the Jagrafess – that is manipulating the broadcasts.

The Doctor realises the Jagrafess needs to be kept cold. He and Rose are captured by the Editor, but they let their new friend Cathica know – and she is able to channel heat up to Floor 500 and destroy the Jagrafess.

Written by
Russell T Davies
Featuring
the Ninth Doctor,
Rose and Adam
First broadcast
7 May 2005
1 episode

SATELLITE FIVE

In this time of the Fourth Great and Bountiful Human Empire, Satellite Five is responsible for broadcasting 600 channels of constant news reports. Satellite Five is where news is gathered, written up, packaged and sold. Nothing happens in the Human Empire without going through Satellite Five.

Floor 500 is the Editorial level – where the management is based – and is the place to which everyone else aspires to be promoted. The walls are rumoured to be made of gold. But the reality is very different – it is cold and dilapidated.

THE EDITOR

Looking like a corporate version of Jack Frost, the Editor lives in the icy environment of Floor 500. He represents a consortium of banks, working directly with the Jagrafess to maximise the banks' profits. Its presence means that there is no war or bloodshed, simply a silent occupation, making it a fairly cheap form of government.

When he discovers the truth about the Doctor and the TARDIS, the Editor sees the possibility of controlling humanity for all time.

ZOMBIES

The Jagrafess controls humanity through computer chips implanted in their heads. This is an extension of the technology the Satellite Five journalists use to gather and broadcast news. Compressed news information is streamed into the brain and the human becomes a part of the analytical software.

The Editor uses drones – animated human corpses – to run his control room on Floor 500. Even though their brains have died, the implanted chips keep working and animate the dead bodies to obey the Editor's commands.

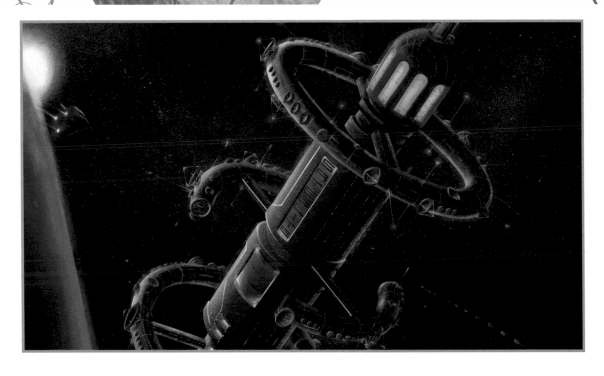

CREATING SATELLITE FIVE

Much of Satellite Five was never actually built; most of the interior and the mighty Jagrafess were computer-generated images (CGI). CGI was also used to create the effect of the chips embedded in people's heads. Here you can see the original design paintings for Satellite Five, as well as the finished computer images of the satellite and the head chip. The Jagrafess CGI was designed and created by The Mill.

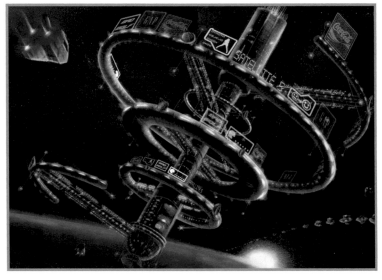

Top and right: Concept paintings of the exterior of Satellite Five. Above: Adam's head chip was a CGI added by The Mill.

Above: The design for the interior of Satellite Five. Right: Satellite Five was a CGI created by The Mill.

Below: An interior design (top) and the finished set (bottom), the upper portion of which is a CGI.

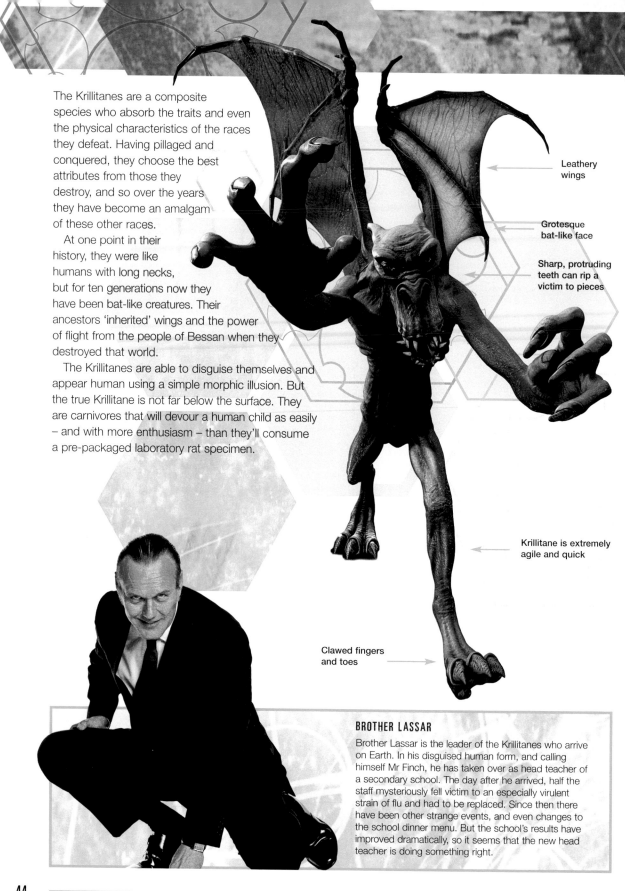

The Krillitanes are a composite species who absorb the traits and even the physical characteristics of the races they defeat. Having pillaged and conquered, they choose the best attributes from those they destroy, and so over the years they have become an amalgam of these other races.

At one point in their history, they were like humans with long necks, but for ten generations now they have been bat-like creatures. Their ancestors 'inherited' wings and the power of flight from the people of Bessan when they destroyed that world.

The Krillitanes are able to disguise themselves and appear human using a simple morphic illusion. But the true Krillitane is not far below the surface. They are carnivores that will devour a human child as easily – and with more enthusiasm – than they'll consume a pre-packaged laboratory rat specimen.

Leathery wings

Grotesque bat-like face

Sharp, protruding teeth can rip a victim to pieces

Krillitane is extremely agile and quick

Clawed fingers and toes

BROTHER LASSAR

Brother Lassar is the leader of the Krillitanes who arrive on Earth. In his disguised human form, and calling himself Mr Finch, he has taken over as head teacher of a secondary school. The day after he arrived, half the staff mysteriously fell victim to an especially virulent strain of flu and had to be replaced. Since then there have been other strange events, and even changes to the school dinner menu. But the school's results have improved dramatically, so it seems that the new head teacher is doing something right.

New head teacher Mr Finch keeps a close eye on things in his school.

SCHOOL REUNION

The Doctor and Rose investigate a school in the middle of a spate of UFO sightings, where exam results have improved dramatically with the arrival of a new head teacher, Finch. With Rose working as a dinner lady and the Doctor as a supply teacher, they meet the Doctor's former companion Sarah Jane Smith, who is also suspicious of events at the school.

In fact Finch is a Krillitane – as are half the staff. They are using Krillitane oil to enhance the mental capacity of the children in the hope of solving the Skasas Paradigm, which will give them control over the universe itself. The Doctor, Rose and Sarah manage to sabotage the plan, and K-9 destroys the store of oil. The Krillitanes are caught in the blast.

Written by
Toby Whithouse
Featuring
the Tenth Doctor, Rose, Mickey, Sarah and K-9
First broadcast
spring 2006
1 episode

THE SCHOOL

The Krillitanes have taken over a secondary school by replacing the head teacher and many of the staff. Mr Finch took over as head teacher three months before the Doctor and Rose's visit, and introduced a new curriculum. This led to a dramatic improvement in the school's results. Despite this success, there is a high turnover of teaching staff, with one teacher being replaced after a winning lottery ticket was pushed through her door.

When Mickey found out over 40 UFO sitings had occurred nearby, he called the Doctor and Rose to investigate.

KRILLITANE OIL

The Krillitanes have changed so far from their original form that they now find their own oil lethally toxic, though it is harmless to humans (and Time Lords). The oil enhances the mental powers of those who consume it. The chips served at school dinners – definitely not a healthy option – are cooked in the oil and improve the abilities of some of the pupils to a point where Finch can use them to calculate the Skasas Paradigm.

But the oil is also highly flammable, and K-9 is able to destroy the school, and the Krillitanes inside, by igniting it.

THE SKASAS PARADIGM

Also known as the 'God Maker' or the 'Universal Theory', the Skasas Paradigm is the key to the way the universe works. Anyone who unravels it can control the very building blocks of time, space and universal matter. But it takes more than just computational power to crack the Paradigm. It also needs imagination – which is why the Krillitanes are using school children to work it out.

Once he knows the solution, Finch believes that the universe itself will be like clay in his hands ... and he tries to persuade the Doctor to join him.

SCRIPTING THE KRILLITANES

The task of creating new aliens to face the Doctor, Rose and Mickey, and bringing back Sarah and K-9, was given to writer Toby Whithouse.

Best known as the creator of the popular Channel 4 comedy drama **No Angels**, Toby was approached to write for **Doctor Who** before the first episode of the 2005 series had even aired. Having renewed his acquaintance with both Sarah and K-9 by watching episodes of the classic series, Toby came up with a story called *Black Ops* that was set in an army camp and surrounding village. On the suggestion of Russell T Davies, he changed the location, and the story became *School Reunion*.

Like the Gelth, the Reapers, and the Jagrafess, the Krillitanes were designed and created entirely as computer-generated images (CGI) by The Mill, and added to the live-action material shot in the studio and on location.

Above: The Krillitanes in their true form.
Right: Rose does not relish her new job as a dinner lady.
Opposite (main pic): Rose and the Doctor seek to thwart Brother Lassar's plans.

SCRIPT EXTRACT

Kenny looks in, spooked, hearing…
A snuffle, a crack of bones. From
the back of the class. In plain
daylight, something hidden, between
the back row of desks and the wall…
Kenny, still at the front, crouches
down, looks…

Right at the back, through all the
chair and desk legs, a black shape.
Shuddering. Breathing like an animal.
And then, still at a distance,
through all the wooden legs –

FX – a terrible BAT FACE turns,
fast, looks at Kenny – !

*Above: Actor Anthony Head gets
into his role as Mr Finch.*
Top left: The Krillitanes asleep in the school.
*Top right: Stunt rats are prepared
for their appearance.*

*Right: Sarah with her best friend, the Fourth
Doctor, in* The Seeds of Doom.
Bottom left: In Planet of the Spiders *Sarah
discovers that attack by giant spiders is just one
hazard of being the Doctor's companion.
Below right: In her final story,* The Hand of Fear,
Sarah is possessed by an alien hand.

SARAH

Sarah Jane Smith was a 23-year-old investigative journalist when she
first encountered the Doctor – in *The Time Warrior* (first broadcast
15 December 1973 – 5 January 1974). Ever on the lookout for a good
story, she took the place of her Aunt Lavinia – a noted scientist – to visit a
research centre, where she met the Doctor. When the Doctor left to follow
kidnapped scientists through time, Sarah
stowed away in the TARDIS – and was
amazed first at its internal dimensions, and
later by arriving back in medieval times. The

Doctor was then in his third
incarnation, working part
time as an adviser to UNIT,
and Sarah – never afraid to
take risks, and determined
to expose the truth in any
situation – soon found herself working with him.

It is Sarah's intelligence, determination, loyalty and
conviction that the Doctor comes to value and admire.
In his fourth incarnation, he describes her not only as
his friend – a rare admission for the Doctor – but as his
best friend. When they are forced to part company as
the Doctor is summoned back to his home planet,
Gallifrey, (in *The Hand of Fear*) both are saddened by
her departure.

In the one-off special **K-9 and Company** (first
broadcast on 28 December 1981), we find out that
the Doctor has left Sarah a present: K-9 Mark III.

In *School Reunion*, we discover that Sarah has never
forgotten, or really moved on from, her time with the
Doctor. But the events of this story, and the time she
spends talking to Rose, enable her to put her time-
travelling into perspective.

K-9

K-9 is a robot computer designed to resemble a dog. The original K-9 was constructed by Professor Marius of the Bi-Al Foundation in the year 5000. Unable to take K-9 home with him to Earth (because of weight restrictions for the journey), the professor offers him to the Doctor, then in his fourth incarnation (in *The Invisible Enemy* – first broadcast 1–22 October 1977).

K-9 can speak, and print data. He has a 'nose-laser' that

emerges from his head and can be set to various levels, enabling him to stun or kill life forms, as well as serving as a cutting tool. Intelligent and with a vast memory, K-9 has an affinity with the TARDIS and learns much from its data banks during his time aboard.

There have been three different 'versions' of K-9. The Doctor left K-9 Mark I with his companion Leela on Gallifrey, while K-9 Mark II went with the Doctor's Time Lord companion Romana into another universe.

The Doctor gave K-9 Mark III to his friend and former companion Sarah Jane Smith – and he is seen with her in *The Five Doctors* (first broadcast in the UK on 25 November 1963) having shared an adventure with her in the spin-off programme **K-9 and Company**.

By the time Sarah meets the Doctor again in *School Reunion*, K-9 is old and dilapidated and has stopped working. The Doctor is able to repair him – and to rebuild him for Sarah when he is all-but destroyed at the end of the story.

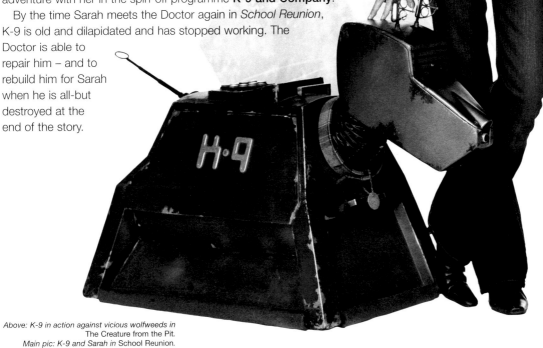

Above: K-9 in action against vicious wolfweeds in
The Creature from the Pit.
Main pic: K-9 and Sarah in School Reunion.

NEW EARTH

By the year five billion, with the original Earth abandoned and destroyed when the sun expanded, the human race has adopted a planet in the galaxy M87 as 'New Earth' – a new home, to satisfy humanity's nostalgia for the old planet.

In many ways, New Earth resembles the original. There is water, blue sky ... corruption. But there are also several moons, and apple-grass grows in the meadows. The massive new mega-cities – like New New York (actually the fifteenth version of the city) – sprawl across the planet's surface.

The cat-like Sisters of Plenitude run the planet's most advanced medical facility, just outside New New York.

NEW EARTH

Arriving on New Earth in response to a message the Doctor receives through his psychic paper, the Doctor and Rose visit a huge hospital complex run by the cat-like Sisters of Plenitude. The message is from the Face of Boe, who seems to be dying, despite the help of the Sisters.

Rose meets another old acquaintance – Cassandra – alive and well, and out for revenge. While Cassandra implants her consciousness inside Rose's body, the Doctor discovers that the miracle treatments the Sisters offer come at a price – a price the Doctor believes is too great. The Doctor must battle to restore Rose to her own body, and to save the hospital from the infected 'patients' that the Sisters have created.

Written by
Russell T Davies
Featuring
the Tenth Doctor
and Rose
First broadcast
spring 2006
1 episode

OTHER WORLDS

Rose has been to several alien worlds with the Doctor. In *Boom Town* she mentions Grajick Major, the Glass Deserts of San Kaloon and Justicia (which also features in the novel *The Monsters Inside*). She tells Mickey about Woman Wept – a world that has a continent shaped like a lamenting woman, where the sea froze in a second.

Among other worlds the Doctor has mentioned to Rose is Barcelona – a planet where the dogs have no noses, so just how *do* they smell?

Top: The Doctor discovers the terrible secret of the Intensive Care Unit.

THE FACE OF BOE

Incredibly old and infinitely wise, the Face of Boe sends the Doctor a message to bring him to New Earth. The Face of Boe is dying – has *decided* to die. It has grown tired of the universe after its long life, but before it dies it must, in accordance with legend, pass on a single great secret to a homeless, wandering traveller, the Lonely God: the Doctor.

But when the Doctor comes to hear the secret, the Face of Boe says that the Doctor has shown it how to look at the universe anew and the secret can wait. They will meet again, for a third and final time, and when that happens the truth – whatever it is – will be told.

Right: Cassandra, the last time she was told she was beautiful.
Below: Cassandra, less beautiful after a spell in the basement.

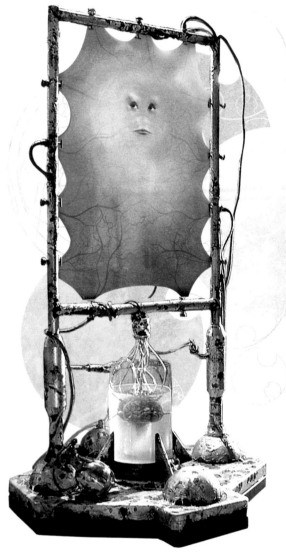

CASSANDRA

After her apparent death on Platform One (in *The End of the World*), Cassandra's brain survived, though her stretched-skin body was dried out and withered. Her eyes were salvaged from a bin, and she rebuilt herself with skin from the back of her original form.

Stowing away on the Face of Boe's life-support system, Cassandra was brought to the hospital on New Earth, where she hides in the basement with her faithful acolyte Chip and steals the medicine she needs to survive.

But when Rose and the Doctor arrive, she devises a new plan – to steal Rose's body and implant her own consciousness inside it. She then tries to blackmail the Sisters of Plenitude, threatening to tell the people of New Earth the truth about how their treatments are derived.

After the Doctor has sorted out the trouble on New Earth, he takes Cassandra back – in Chip's dying body – to her own past, to the last time she was truly happy: a drinks party for the Ambassador of Thrace, which was the last occasion when someone told her she was beautiful.

CHIP

Cassandra's loyal servant Chip is actually a force-grown clone. Cassandra has modelled him on the last person who ever told her she was beautiful.

In fact, this encounter was a self-fulfilling prophecy and a time paradox. It is Cassandra herself, inside Chip's body, that the Doctor takes back to tell her earlier self that she is beautiful. So Cassandra later models the cloned Chip on himself, as she saw him at the party.

THE SISTERS OF PLENITUDE

The huge medical facility outside New New York is run by the Sisters of Plenitude. They are cat-like beings, who take a life-long vow to help others and to minister to and heal the sick. Humanity poses a challenge for them, as humans are afflicted with so many diseases.

Within the hospital, the Sisters can, miraculously, cure even the most virulent and previously untreatable diseases and conditions. These include:

Petrifold Regression – in which the patient literally turns to stone,
Marconi's Disease – treated on New Earth using a unique cell-washing cascade,
Pallidome Pancrosis – which usually kills the victim within ten minutes.

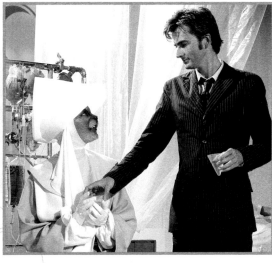

There is even a unit specialising in nano-dentistry. But the one thing the Sisters of Plenitude cannot cure is old age.

And, as the Doctor discovers, the treatments the Sisters administer are based on a terrible, dark secret that festers at the heart of their hospital…

Above: The Doctor gives advice on treatment.
Left: The Sisters of Plenitude provide medical facilities for the citizens of New Earth.

Left: A completed mask for Jatt, ready to be applied to the actress's face.

SCRIPT EXTRACT

NUNS – The SISTERS OF PLENITUDE – glide to and fro, in flowing cream robes and formal headgear, their faces concealed behind veils…

SISTERS are hurrying towards him, led by MATRON CASP. As she approaches, she lifts her veil. The Sisters are CATS; beautiful, but with that cool feline archness, too.

MAKING THE SISTERS

The original designs for the faces of the Sisters of Plenitude were painted over photographs of the actresses chosen to play the roles. Millennium FX made the final masks, based on an agreed design, using a process that punches tiny filaments of flock-like material through a thin latex face mask. They took a mould of each actress's face, and individually tailored the masks to fit.

The finished products were then fixed in position and blended with make-up to create the final impressive appearance of the cat people. The masks themselves were so thin and delicate that they could only be used once – the process of removing the mask at the end of the day in effect destroyed it. So a new mask was needed for each character every day.

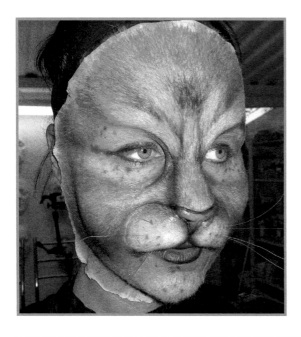

Left: Jatt's mask is tested to ensure it fits perfectly.
Above: An early design for more 'alien' cat people, by Millennium FX.

THE 'PATIENTS'

The Sisters of Plenitude hide a terrible secret – the truth behind their ability to cure any disease. Sick patients are stored in the Intensive Care Unit of the New Earth hospital. But these are not people who have caught diseases or been taken ill and need treatment. These are specially grown humans who have been deliberately infected with every known disease and illness, so as to make them living incubators for the vaccines and cures the Sisters use. Because they are the carriers of the diseases, they do not die from them. The Sisters have experimented with clone-meat and biocattle, but human flesh is the only environment in which the diseases can be cultivated successfully and quickly.

The patients are kept in individual booths, sealed from the outside world, fed with pipes bearing nutrients and oxygen … and more disease. They are perpetually unconscious – and the ultimate research laboratory.

But the patients are not as insensitive and ignorant as many of the Sisters believe. Sister Corvin has written a thesis that suggests that sentience might migrate to these bodies, but the policy of Matron Casp is to incinerate any of these patients who show signs of real life.

Once released from their cubicles, the patients only want affection. But in the sterile atmosphere, their very touch is fatal, and the Doctor must devise a cure, while staying away from them long enough to administer it.

Top: The patients escape from 'Intensive Care'.
Above: The Doctor, Chip and Rose watch in horror.

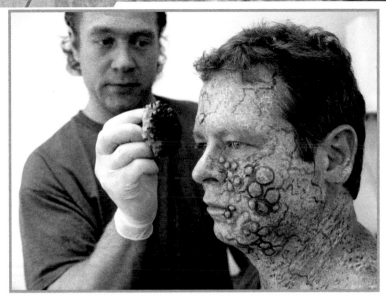

Right: A patient gets treatment from the make-up department.

INFECTING THE PATIENTS

The infected Patients kept in the 'Intensive Care' Unit by the Sisters were created using a combination of prosthetics and conventional make-up techniques. While they were to appear horrific, the Patients are tragic, sympathetic characters in the story and not really monsters as such, so they needed to appear grotesque without being overtly monstrous.

Another consideration the production team had was that, given the age range of the audience, they did not want the make-up to be too horrific or extreme for younger and more sensitive viewers. So the initial design ideas were toned down to avoid showing blood or open wounds, or too much gory red. Getting the right balance and making the Patients frightening without being horrific was a difficult challenge, but one that the prosthetics, make-up and costume design teams rose to magnificently, as the images on this page show.

SCRIPT EXTRACT

FX: WIDE SHOT, the Doctor and Rose's gantry just one level of many; rows above, rows below, connected by metal staircases. Booth after booth after booth, very Borg ship.

CUT TO the Doctor, using the sonic screwdriver on a booth's locking bolt. *Click*!, and he heaves the door open.

The PATIENT is a sick Human. Wearing a simple, dirty-grey tunic. Every inch of skin is flaky, mottled, dirty, wet. Immobile, but the eyes are alive, scared.

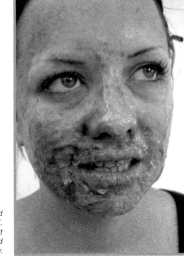

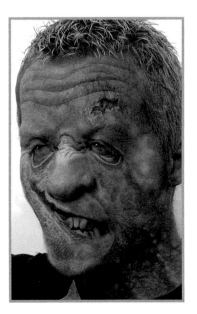

Right: A make-up test conducted by Millennium FX.
Far right: An early design – it was decided that the distorted features were too horrific and did not engender sympathy.

Omega was the Time Lord who gave his people the power to travel in time, through a fantastic feat of solar engineering. Using a remote stellar manipulator, nicknamed the Hand of Omega, he blew up a star. Legend says that Omega was lost in the explosion, but in fact he was sucked into the resulting black hole, where he continued to exist in an antimatter world he controlled using the forces contained in the black hole. He was unable to escape as his will held this world together. He felt that he'd been abandoned by the Time Lords and eventually sought to drain all their power in revenge.

The mask was designed to protect Omega from the corrosive effect of the singularity light beam that powers his world, but the corrosion has already taken place, and beneath the mask he does not exist

Omega is, arguably, the first-ever Time Lord

Omega's costume changed between *The Three Doctors* (above) and *Arc of Infinity* (right). Since it is a product of his will, he can wear whatever he imagines

OMEGA

The Second and Third Doctors meet Omega.

THE THREE DOCTORS

Written by
Bob Baker and Dave Martin
Featuring
the First, Second and Third
Doctors, UNIT and Jo
First broadcast
30 December 1972 –
20 January 1973
4 episodes

With their power over time being drained away through a mysterious black hole, the Time Lords send the first three incarnations of the Doctor to investigate. They travel through the black hole and battle Omega in a world of antimatter. Omega wants the Doctor to take his place so he can escape from his world. But the Doctors discover that Omega has long since died, and only his will lives on.

ARC OF INFINITY

In a later attempt to escape, Omega plans to 'bond' with a Time Lord and assume their form – and he has the bio-data information he needs on the Doctor. To prevent this, the Time Lords try to execute the Doctor. But he escapes and unmasks the traitor in the High Council of Time Lords who has been helping Omega. The Doctor travels to Amsterdam, where he is able finally to defeat Omega.

Written by
Johnny Byrne
Featuring
the Fifth Doctor,
Nyssa and Tegan
First broadcast
3 January 1983 –
12 January 1983
4 episodes

GELL GUARDS

Created by Omega from the 'raw stuff of matter', so they can exist in the real universe and Omega's black hole, the Gell Guards are Omega's servants in his bleak world of antimatter. They can fire explosive bolts from their claws. Omega sends Gell Guards, together with another gelatinous organism, to Earth to kidnap the Third Doctor from UNIT headquarters.

THE ERGON

The Fifth Doctor tactfully describes the Ergon as one of Omega's 'less successful attempts at psychosynthesis'. Omega uses the Ergon as his agent on Earth when he arrives in Amsterdam and attempts to steal the Doctor's bio-data so he can exist in the real universe once more.

The Rani is a renegade Time Lord. She is a brilliant chemist, as well as being adept in other areas of science. She was exiled by the Time Lords after one of her experiments on mice turned them into monsters, resulting in an unfortunate incident with the President's cat. In the Doctor's opinion, the Time Lords should never have exiled the Rani, but locked her in a padded cell instead.

Ruler of planets such as Miasimia Goria and later Lakertya, the unscrupulous Rani sees their inhabitants merely as subjects for her experiments.

Beautiful but deadly

Rani dresses glamorously when not in disguise

Bracelet contains capsules and tablets

THE RANI'S TARDIS

The Rani's TARDIS, unlike the Doctor's, can still disguise itself to blend in with its surroundings using its Chameleon Circuit. In *The Mark of the Rani* it is disguised as a cupboard, while in *Time and the Rani* it appears as a reflective pyramid.

The Doctor opens the Rani's TARDIS with his own TARDIS key, but the internal design is different from the Doctor's TARDIS – it is dark, with a round console. It is linked to a Stattenheim remote control. The Doctor is able to sabotage the Rani's TARDIS by resetting the navigational system and velocity regulator.

THE RANI

Disguised as an old woman, the Rani is after human brain fluid.

THE MARK OF THE RANI

Written by
Pip and Jane Baker
Featuring
the Sixth Doctor
and Peri
First broadcast
2 February 1985 –
9 February 1985
2 episodes

The Doctor and Peri arrive in Killingworth, where George Stephenson is organising a meeting of the greatest British thinkers and engineers. The Master is seeking revenge on the Doctor after the Doctor abandoned him to die on the planet Sarn, and also plans to take control of the great thinkers and manipulate them to turn Earth into a power base.

But the Rani is in Killingworth, too. She is extracting fluid from people's brains, making them unnaturally aggressive.

The Doctor manages to sabotage the Rani's TARDIS, so that she and the Master are trapped inside it when it suffers time spillage – alongside an embryo tyrannosaurus, which starts to grow…

BRAIN FLUID

The Rani's plan is to use the fluid she extracts from her victims' brains to keep her own alien subjects on Miasimia Goria placid, but in the process of heightening their awareness, she reduces her subjects' ability to sleep, making them aggressive and difficult to control.

She has been coming to Earth for centuries, using various events in history as cover, including the Trojan Wars, the Dark Ages, the American War of Independence and – as seen in this story – the Luddite riots.

BOOBY TRAPS

The Rani lays mines that turn anyone who steps on them – including the unfortunate Luke Ward, Stephenson's assistant – into a tree. She argues that she's improving their lifespan (but presumably not their social life).

The Rani's TARDIS is protected by a mustard-gas booby trap hidden in a Turner painting on a screen.

In *Time and the Rani* she has set traps that enclose the victim in a bubble that spins off, then explodes when it lands (unless it lands on water – which is how Mel is able to escape).

SHEER BLIST

The location used as Killingworth was Blists Hill Open Air Museum at Ironbridge Gorge in Shropshire. The story included a larger amount of location filming than was usual, which enhanced the atmosphere and apparent authenticity of the historical setting. But because of rain, the crew, led by director Sarah Hellings, was unable to finish the job, and some sequences, including the Doctor escaping, were shot at a different wood.

The two Mels – the Doctor is confused as the Rani disguises herself as his companion.

TIME AND THE RANI

The Rani attacks the TARDIS, causing the Doctor to regenerate. She has taken over the planet Lakertya with alien Tetraps as her henchmen. Using the combined talents of various geniuses she has taken from throughout history – including Einstein and, she hopes, the Doctor – the Rani plans to create a time manipulator. She has built a missile to fire at an asteroid composed of strange matter, creating a chain reaction to power the device. As a side effect, the peaceful people of Lakertya will be destroyed, but the Rani isn't about to let a little thing like genocide put her off. The newly regenerated Doctor recovers in time to help Mel thwart the Rani's plans, and the Rani is captured by the Tetraps.

Written by
Pip and Jane Baker
Featuring
the Seventh Doctor
and Mel
First broadcast
7 September 1987 –
28 September 1987
4 episodes

LAKERTYA

The Lakertyans are humanoid with reptilian influences, including a crest that is part of their skull. They relax at their Centre of Leisure – where the Rani releases killer insects from a spinning ball.

The Rani holds the Lakertyan leader Beyus hostage, together with Sarn, his daughter, (who is killed by a bubble trap when trying to escape). Beyus sacrifices himself helping the Doctor to thwart the Rani's plan. He stays in her lab to ensure the success of the Doctor's sabotage of the huge brain she has built to house the collective genius she has gathered.

TETRAPS

The Tetraps are large, bat-like creatures from the planet Tetrapyriarbus. They sleep hanging upside-down in a cavern, and feed on a dark sludge supplied down a chute into a trough. The Tetraps have four eyes, one on each side of their head. They hunt with guns that fire nets that cover and incapacitate their prey.

When the Tetrap leader, overhears the Rani's plan, he realises that he and his people will be killed on Lakertya when the time manipulator is created. Enraged, the Tetraps capture the Rani in her own TARDIS.

DISGUISES

In *The Mark of the Rani,* the Rani disguises herself as an elderly lady who runs a bathhouse where the miners can clean up as they come off duty from the pits. She is then able to gas them, and remove their brain fluid while they are unconscious.

In *Time and the Rani,* she pretends to be the Doctor's companion Mel – complete with a costume and red wig – in order to get the Doctor's cooperation. Later she creates a hologram of Mel that fools the Doctor into returning a vital component.

The Reapers are creatures that take advantage of wounds in time – places where time itself has been damaged in some way. They are drawn to the wound, like bacteria. But unlike bacteria they sterilise the wound – by destroying everything inside it.

The Reapers destroy the newest objects and people first, working back through history until the entire affected, infected world is destroyed. Before the Great Time War the Time Lords would intervene to mitigate the Reapers' behaviour. But now that the Time Lords are gone, and there is no defence against them, the Reapers ravage time unchecked.

Scythe-like tail

The Reaper consumes its victims when it attacks, so they cease to exist

Sharp claws can rip through stone

Scaled, armoured, protective skin

Hideous bat-like wings

WOUNDED TIME

Rose changes history by saving her father, Pete Tyler, from being run down and killed by a car. The moment of Pete Tyler's death was a vulnerable point in time because of the presence there of two versions of the Doctor and Rose. Rose's action further weakens space and time, and the Reapers are able to break through into reality to sterilise the wound by consuming everything in the affected area … everything on Earth.

A terrifying Reaper appears in the church.

FATHER'S DAY

The Doctor agrees to take Rose back to 1987 to witness her father's death in a hit-and-run accident. But Rose saves her father's life. The Doctor is irate, but his anger turns to concern as Reapers take advantage of the change in history and start to attack. Under siege with a wedding party in the local church, the Doctor hopes to use the TARDIS to heal the wound and restore normality, leaving Rose's dad alive.

But a Reaper breaks into the church. It consumes the Doctor and breaks the link he has set up with the TARDIS. Pete is able to put history back on track – bringing back the Doctor and the other victims of the Reapers – by throwing himself under the car that originally killed him…

Written by
Paul Cornell
Featuring
the Ninth Doctor
and Rose
First broadcast
14 May 2005
1 episode

PETE TYLER

Pete Tyler died on 7 November 1987, on his way to the wedding of Stuart Hoskins and Sarah Clark, after going to buy them a vase as a present. He was hit by a car, and died at the scene. But Rose intervenes and saves him, causing a paradox and the appearance of the Reapers.

Eventually, Pete realises what he must do to end the paradox and heal the wound in time – sacrificing the life he has just regained to save Rose, Jackie, the Doctor and everyone else.

EMPTY TARDIS

Affected by the paradox and the damage done to time itself, the TARDIS becomes a normal police box – the interior being thrown out of the infected area. When the Doctor opens the doors he finds the TARDIS interior is gone, leaving just an empty shell.

The TARDIS key glows hot to tell the Doctor it is still connected to the TARDIS, even though it seems to have gone. But the connection is broken by a Reaper. When the effects of the paradox are reversed, the TARDIS returns to normal.

PARADOXES

One example of a time paradox is the 'Grandfather Paradox' – when someone goes back in time and kills their own grandfather. This means they could not then have existed to go back and kill their grandfather, but that means the grandfather is not dead so the killing could have taken place after all…

In *Day of the Daleks*, the Doctor mentions the Blinovitch Limitation Effect. It defines a link between different times: guerrillas fighting the Daleks cannot keep going back to the same point in time but only a time relative to their own.

SCRIPTING THE REAPERS

Writer Paul Cornell was already well known to **Doctor Who** fans having written several novels, and having scripted (and novelised) the BBCi webcast *Scream of the Shalka* – an animated adventure starring Richard E. Grant as a new Doctor. He has written mainstream science fiction, comic strips and audio drama and is also an established script writer, whose credits include **Casualty**, **Holby City** and **Children's Ward**.

Paul was delighted to be asked to write a script for the new series of **Doctor Who**. Here he describes the Reapers and their function in the universe:

'The Reapers are naturally occurring predatory animals that live in the Space–Time Vortex. Glimpses of them may have helped to form Earth legends of the "grim reaper". When the Time Lords kept a check on time-faring creatures, a barrier prevented the Reapers from feeding on intelligent species. But now the Time Lords are gone, a large change in time made at a weak point (such as when two copies of the same person are present) can sometimes weaken the universe to such an extent that the Reapers swarm in from the Vortex.

'Their feeding process, consuming every living thing (their favourite dish being the youngest), acts as a natural part of the ecology of time. It prevents changes caused by time travel from spiralling into universe-wide changes in history, a function that, while they existed, the Time Lords themselves took on.'

Top left: A Reaper attacks the church.
Above (top): The Doctor runs to save Rose.
Above (bottom): Behind the scenes – falling on to crash-mats.
Left: The Doctor realises the danger.

CREATING THE REAPERS

The original idea for the design of the Reapers was that they should be cloaked, humanoid figures with scythes – not unlike the classic image of the figure of Death. But as ideas progressed, this was abandoned in favour of a more alien creature. Shown here is an early design drawing, along with a shot of the finished creature from the episode itself.

The Reapers, never actually named within the story, were designed and created entirely as computer-generated images (CGI) by The Mill, and added into live-action footage shot on location in Cardiff.

SCRIPT EXTRACT

THE DOCTOR
Rose! Get in the church!

Which she does hear. She turns with a big smile of relief, she knew he'd come after her!

She turns round and sees a floating shape materialising overhead. She stares. And screams.

We see what's looming over her.
It's a REAPER.

Its shape keeps shifting, juddering, superimposed on itself like something out of *Jacob's Ladder*, shrieking its alien sound.

Top: An early design idea for the Reaper.
Left: A Reaper engulfs its victim.

THE SANDMINER ROBOTS

The robots that the Fourth Doctor and Leela find operating a huge Sandminer on a distant planet are stylised humanoids, identified by type and number, programmed to obey the human crew and perform menial tasks. Each Voc class robot has over a million multi-level constrainers, which prevent it from being able to harm humans. But, as the Doctor and Leela discover, someone has learned how to override these constraints and the robots have got more than cleaning on their minds.

The robots are controlled by a silver Super Voc, in this case SV7. It controls the other robots, acting as their coordinator and relaying all commands.

The golden Voc robots, all numbered with a V prefix, are intelligent, with a degree of self-control. They can also speak, and have a certain amount of initiative.

The dark-coloured Dum robots are single-function robots used for simple labour tasks. They are all numbered with a D prefix and cannot speak.

Robots are incredibly strong

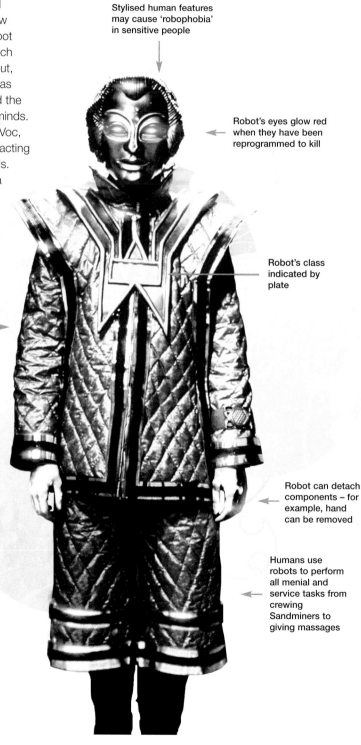

Stylised human features may cause 'robophobia' in sensitive people

Robot's eyes glow red when they have been reprogrammed to kill

Robot's class indicated by plate

Robot can detach components – for example, hand can be removed

Humans use robots to perform all menial and service tasks from crewing Sandminers to giving massages

CORPSE MARKERS

Faulty robots are deactivated and must be returned to a construction centre for reactivation. They are marked with red robot-deactivation discs, which the workers call 'corpse markers'.

Three Voc robots prepare to attack.

THE ROBOTS OF DEATH

The Doctor and Leela arrive on a Sandminer where the crew believe them to be responsible for a murder. The alternative – that one of the robots on board is responsible – is too terrible to contemplate. But also on board is an undercover operative from the mining company and a disguised robot detective, D84. They are looking for mad scientist – and 'boring maniac' – Taren Capel, who has threatened to reprogramme robots to kill people and take over the world.

With most of the crew dead, and the robots in open rebellion, Taren Capel reveals himself and the Doctor is forced to take drastic action.

Written by
Chris Boucher
Featuring
the Fourth Doctor and Leela
First broadcast
29 January 1977 –
19 February 1977
4 episodes

THE SANDMINER

Storm Mine Four travels over the vast desert, extracting valuable ores and minerals from the shifting sands. The Sandminer is commanded by Uvanov. The human crew includes: Pilot Toos; Chief Mover Poul (an undercover agent for the company, who has robophobia); the impetuous Mover Borg; Chief Fixer Dask; Cass; Kerril; Zilda; and government meteorologist Chub.

While the robots can mine without human supervision, their lack of instincts means they are less efficient at tracing and following ore streams.

TAREN CAPEL

Raised by robots from birth, Taren Capel believes that it is his mission to free his 'brother' robots from human bondage. He has taken the place of a member of the Sandminer's crew in order to convert robots to kill humans. When he orders the death of a human, Capel hands the robot a corpse marker to place on the body.

The robots identify humans in their command circuit by voice. When Taren Capel's voice is altered by helium, SV7 does not recognise him and obeying his command to 'kill all humans', kills Capel.

D84

D84 is a disguised Voc or Super Voc working with Poul to check whether Taren Capel is aboard the Sandminer. While the robots are said not to have feelings, D84 strikes up a relationship with the Doctor and ultimately sacrifices himself to destroy the converted robots.

The Doctor is able to create a 'final deactivator' tuned into Taren Capel's robot command circuit. Wounded by a Laserson Probe wielded by one of Capel's homicidal robots, D84 activates the device, destroying all of Capel's robots except SV7.

SCAROTH

Distinctive alien skin ripples and twitches

Scaroth's true face (usually concealed behind tight-fitting mask)

Scaroth has many human guises, including Captain Tancredi

Jagaroth are humanoid in shape

Cravat conceals bottom of human face mask

Beneath body suit, skin is similar texture to head

The Doctor describes the Jagaroth as a 'vicious, callous, warlike race'. They existed millions of years ago, and all but one of the Jagaroth were killed when their spaceship exploded while trying to take off from prehistoric Earth.

Scaroth was the pilot of that ship, and the only survivor; splintered into 12 aspects of himself, scattered throughout Earth's history and living independent but connected lives – each aspect is identical, but none is complete.

Scaroth claims he helped Man discover fire, invent the wheel, map the heavens and build the pyramids … always working to advance human evolution to a point where the technology he needs is available to his self furthest in the future – Count Scarlioni, in Paris, 1979.

THE JAGAROTH SPACESHIP

For *City of Death*, visual-effects designer Ian Scoones was keen to develop the design of primeval Earth for his model shot of the Jagaroth spaceship exploding, rather than match his model to a studio set. He created a detailed picture of what he intended to build, and in agreement with set designer Richard McManan-Smith, built a large, detailed model.

City of Death opens with an impressive shot of the primeval landscape, culminating with the appearance of Scaroth's spider-like spaceship. This sequence, including the spaceship taking off, 'warping' and then exploding, was one of the most impressive model sequences achieved on **Doctor Who** up until that time, and remains just as spectacular today.

Scaroth in the warp control cabin of the Jagaroth spaceship.

CITY OF DEATH

Arriving in Paris in 1979, the Doctor and Romana experience strange ripples in time. The culprit is Count Scarlioni, who is financing experiments to roll back time – and who has a wonderfully violent butler. Realising that the Count is planning to steal the *Mona Lisa*, the Doctor and Romana join forces with Duggan, a private detective hired to protect the painting.

They discover that Scarlioni is selling art treasures to finance the time experiments. He plans to take the world back to the moment he tried to lift off in his ship, and warn himself of what will happen. But the Doctor realises that the ship exploding provided the burst of energy that created life on Earth, and Duggan thwarts Scaroth's plans with a timely punch.

Written by
David Agnew
Featuring
the Fourth Doctor
and Romana
First broadcast
29 September 1979 –
20 October 1979
4 episodes

TIME EXPERIMENTS

Scaroth, in the guise of Count Scarlioni, has hired the brilliant Professor Kerensky to work out how he can travel back in time to save himself. Kerensky experiments with eggs to take them forward in time to become live chickens. He can also wind time back so the chicken returns to being an egg. But he can only manipulate time within the 'bubble' he creates that contains the egg/chicken.

Scaroth needs Kerensky to find a way to interact with events in the time bubble – so that Scaroth can intervene to save himself in prehistoric times.

THE *MONA LISA*

In 1505, Captain Tancredi – an aspect of Scaroth – persuades Leonardo da Vinci to paint six copies of the *Mona Lisa*, which he hides for Scarlioni to find in 1979. Scarlioni can then steal the original from the Louvre in 1979, and secretly sell all seven. This will bring in enough money to finance Kerensky's time experiments.

Realising Scarlioni's plan, the Doctor travels back to 1505 and leaves a subtle message – 'This is a fake' – in felt pen on the boards that Leonardo will use, so the copies will be identified.

DUGGAN

Duggan is a private detective hired by a group of art collectors to keep watch on Count Scarlioni. Recently, many valuable art treasures have come on the market, and they seem to have originated with Scarlioni. The feeling is that they must be – excellent – forgeries. In fact they are originals accumulated by the various aspects of Scaroth through the ages.

Duggan soon realises that Scarlioni is intending to steal the *Mona Lisa*. Duggan's philosophy is 'if it moves, hit it', which is just as well, as he saves all life on Earth when he punches Scaroth.

SIL AND THE MENTORS

The planet Thoros-Beta, with its pink water and pale-green sky, is the home of the Mentors. They are led by Lord Kiv, and driven by the desire to make money. The Mentors have enslaved the Alphans – the humanoid inhabitants of Thoros-Alpha.

Sil is a particularly sycophantic and repugnant Mentor. He is sent to Varos to negotiate the yearly price review for Galatron Mining prior to a new contract. Galatron has been buying from Varos – and exploiting the inhabitants – for centuries. With a penchant for marsh minnows, and a constant need to be moisturised in Varos's atmosphere, Sil also has eccentric speech patterns, due to a fault in his language transposer.

Sil is moved around and moisturised by attendants

Slippery slimy skin

Voice translator unit allows Sil to communicate.

Tasty marsh minnows provide sustenance

Tail used to include sting

VAROS

Varos is in the constellation of Cetes and is the only known source of the rare ore Zeiton-7. Over two hundred years ago, it was a prison colony for the criminally insane, and now the descendants of the officer elite still hold power.

The Governor is chosen at random from 12 senior officers and must propose solutions to Varos's problems. These are then put to a public vote and the Governor is subjected to a potentially lethal cell bombardment if he loses.

Torture and execution are carried out in the Punishment Dome. The whole dome is covered by cameras. Varos sells tapes of what happens in the Punishment Dome, as well as broadcasting the events, to divert questions and thoughts of discontent and revolution.

The Doctor confronts Sil on his home planet of Thoros-Beta.

VENGEANCE ON VAROS

Written by
Philip Martin
Featuring
the Sixth Doctor
and Peri
First broadcast
19 January 1985 –
26 January 1985
2 episodes

The TARDIS 'stalls' and only has enough power to get to Varos – an ex-prison planet that is the sole source of the valuable Zeiton-7 needed for repairs. The TARDIS arrives in the Punishment Dome and the Doctor and Peri find themselves trying to escape the tortures and challenges of the Dome on live television.

Meanwhile, the fair but strict Governor of Varos tries to negotiate a higher price for Zeiton-7 with Sil, a representative of the Galatron Mining Corporation, which has led Varos to believe that Zeiton-7 is worthless. The Doctor and Peri join forces with rebel leader Jondar to help the Governor break free of dependence on Sil and the Mentors.

THE TRIAL OF A TIME LORD – MINDWARP

The Doctor is put on trial by his own people, and the events of *Mindwarp* form part of the evidence against him…

Tracing a high-tech weapon to Sil's home planet of Thoros-Beta, the Doctor and Peri find a sea monster biologically upgraded to operate sophisticated machinery, and a creature that is part-man, part-wolf. Human scientist Crozier is experimenting on the native Alphans for the Mentor leader Kiv, to find a way for him to survive as his brain grows too big for his body. With the Doctor apparently cooperating with the Mentors and turning on Peri, events play out to a tragic conclusion.

Written by
Philip Martin
Featuring
the Sixth Doctor
and Peri
First broadcast
4 October 1986 –
25 October 1986
4 episodes

SUTEKH

From the planet Phaester Osiris, Sutekh is the last survivor of the Osirans – a devious and cunning race. He is a force for evil who destroyed his own planet and was finally caught on Earth by the surviving Osirans led by Horus. Once defeated, Sutekh was imprisoned beneath a pyramid, unable to move. The power source for his prison was the Eye of Horus, housed in another pyramid on Mars.

But when Egyptologist Marcus Scarman finds Sutekh's 'tomb', the last surviving Osiran is able to use his immense mental powers to control Scarman and make him use Osiran service robots to build a missile that will destroy the Pyramid of Mars and free Sutekh from his ancient bonds.

Mask covers Osiran jackal-like head

Eyes glow when Sutekh uses his immense mental powers

Sutekh is unable to move until the Eye of Horus is destroyed

Osiran costume and style formed the basis for Ancient Egyptian design

THE OSIRANS

Seven thousand years ago, Sutekh (also known as Set or Seth) destroyed his own planet, Phaester Osiris, and left a trail of havoc across half the galaxy. Horus and the 740 other surviving Osirans finally cornered Sutekh in ancient Egypt, where their conflict became the basis for the ancient Egyptian myths and religion.

SERVICE ROBOT MUMMIES

Sutekh's mummy servants are actually Osiran service robots. Their bindings are chemically impregnated to protect them from damage and corrosion. They are activated and controlled by servants of Sutekh using an ancient ring, which draws power from Sutekh's tomb. Sutekh himself and Marcus Scarman can control the mummies directly by mental force. The instructions are channelled into a pyramid in the small of the mummy's back, but an etheric impulse projected along the right wavelength can block this control.

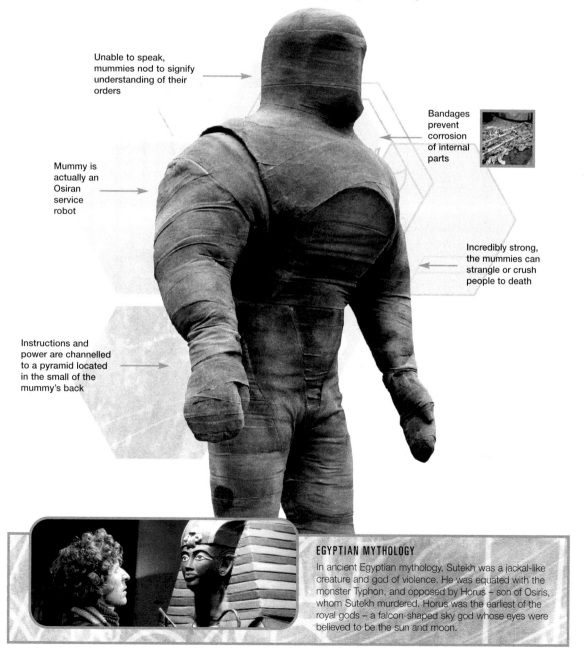

Unable to speak, mummies nod to signify understanding of their orders

Bandages prevent corrosion of internal parts

Mummy is actually an Osiran service robot

Incredibly strong, the mummies can strangle or crush people to death

Instructions and power are channelled to a pyramid located in the small of the mummy's back

EGYPTIAN MYTHOLOGY

In ancient Egyptian mythology, Sutekh was a jackal-like creature and god of violence. He was equated with the monster Typhon, and opposed by Horus – son of Osiris, whom Sutekh murdered. Horus was the earliest of the royal gods – a falcon-shaped sky god whose eyes were believed to be the sun and moon.

SUTEKH AND THE MUMMIES

Osiran service robots guard Sutekh's pyramid missile.

PYRAMIDS OF MARS

Written by
Stephen Harris
Featuring
the Fourth Doctor
and Sarah
First broadcast
25 October 1975 –
15 November 1975
4 episodes

The TARDIS is drawn off course and materialises in 1911 (one of the Doctor's favourite years) in an old priory, where the Osiran Sutekh is using Egyptologist Marcus Scarman to build a missile. The missile will free Sutekh from the Eye of Horus, which holds him prisoner beneath a pyramid in Egypt.

Captured and controlled by Sutekh, the Doctor is forced to take the TARDIS to the Pyramid of Mars, where Sutekh is finally freed by Scarman. But the Doctor is able to return to Earth and defeat Sutekh in the short time it takes before the control cuts out.

THE PYRAMID OF MARS

When he built the Pyramid of Mars to house the Eye of Horus that holds Sutekh prisoner, Horus included many traps and puzzles that have to be solved in order to progress through the pyramid. In addition to getting past booby-trapped doorways and mathematical puzzles linked to explosives, the Doctor must solve a riddle to release Sarah from a trap – if he gets it wrong she will be condemned to instant death.

The mummies that guard the tomb are loyal to Horus and are differentiated from Sutekh's servicers by gold bands.

MARCUS SCARMAN

Marcus Scarman – fellow of All Souls College, professor of archaeology and member of the Royal Society – has disappeared on his expedition to a pyramid near Sakkhara. In fact Scarman was killed by Sutekh when he entered his tomb. His cadaver was animated by Sutekh's will and sent back to the Priory where he lives to supervise the building of the missile that will destroy the Pyramid of Mars.

Scarman's face turns into that of Sutekh as he concentrates to destroy the Eye of Horus.

WRAPPING UP

The costumes for the mummies were designed by Barbara Kidd, and were in several separate pieces – pre-wrapped arms and legs (in two pieces), with the head worn like a helmet and two main body sections. The actors were able to see out through a slit covered by a thin bandage. They found moving through the woods especially tricky because of the uneven ground.

The location for the house and the woods was Stargrove Manor in Hampshire.

An ancient race of honourable warriors, the Sycorax travel through space in their distinctive, angular, rock-like spaceships, conquering planets and enslaving their inhabitants. While they follow an ancient warrior tradition, they prefer to take planets without a fight, tricking world leaders into surrendering their people into slavery and their worlds into bondage.

The Sycorax answer to a single leader, chosen by right of combat and strength. Their ships are more like ancient caves than technological equipment, and are decorated with trophies of their past conquests. Their voices are guttural growls, brutally savage, and their mantra is 'Sycorax strong! Sycorax mighty! Sycorax rock!'

Hideous face is hidden beneath ceremonial helmet crafted from bone

Back-lit eye shields strike fear into enemies

Teeth from defeated enemies

Flexible gauntlets offer protection and allow dexterity

Body armour is covered with robes of office and rank

Ornate wooden staff hung with trophies

Ceremonial broadsword used in challenges of honour and sanctified combat

The Doctor does battle with the Sycorax leader: the prize – planet Earth.

THE CHRISTMAS INVASION

Written by
Russell T Davies
Featuring
theTenth Doctor, Rose,
Jackie and Mickey
First broadcast
25 December 2005
A 60-minute
Christmas Special

The TARDIS crash-lands in London at Christmas, but the Doctor is left unconscious after his regeneration. Rose and Mickey barely escape an attack by a group of homicidal robotic Santas and are attacked by a Christmas tree back at Jackie's flat. The Doctor wakes for long enough to save them – and warn them of a greater threat approaching Earth.

A Sycorax spaceship arrives over London, and the aliens demand that Harriet Jones (Prime Minister) surrenders. With a third of the Earth's population hypnotised into walking to the edge of high buildings and preparing to leap to their deaths, the Doctor must challenge the Sycorax leader to a duel – with planet Earth as the stake.

BLOOD CONTROL

Using a sample of blood from the captured British space probe *Guinevere One*, the Sycorax are able to control all people who have the same blood type (A+). They force the controlled people to stand at the edge of high buildings, and if half the Earth's population is not surrendered into slavery, the Sycorax will ensure the controlled people jump to their deaths. However the Doctor proves the human survival instinct is simply too strong for the victims to be persuaded to kill themselves, and breaks the Sycorax control.

HARRIET JONES (PRIME MINISTER)

Harriet Jones is now prime minister, after her party won a landslide majority at the last election. She rose to power after helping the Doctor to thwart the attempted Slitheen invasion of Earth.

Taking control, Harriet Jones goes to UNIT's secret headquarters under the Tower of London to manage the Sycorax crisis. After witnessing the barbarity of the aliens, she has their retreating ship destroyed using recovered alien technology controlled by the ultra-secret 'Torchwood'. The Doctor is appalled at her actions and vows to see her toppled from power.

THE GRASKE

At about the same time as defeating the Sycorax, the Doctor also thwarted an attempt by the evil Graske of Griffoth to replace Earth's population with their own people (in an interactive adventure for digital TV viewers, *Attack of the Graske*). He travelled to Griffoth with a new human companion (the viewer), who worked out how to gain access to the Graske control area, and reset their teleport equipment, returning the kidnapped humans and representatives of other races to their rightful time and place in history.

THE 'PILOT FISH'

Hitching a ride with the Sycorax spaceship, the creatures the Doctor describes as 'Pilot Fish' arrive on Earth ahead of the Sycorax. They are drawn by the residual energy left in the Doctor following his regeneration. Seeming to sense that Rose, Mickey and Jackie have been with the Doctor, they try to eliminate them first.

The exact nature of these creatures is not revealed, but they are possibly mechanical as the Doctor suggests they want his energy to recharge their batteries. Sensing the festive season in which they arrive, they manifest themselves on Earth as macabre Santa robots and a dangerous Christmas tree that spins at speed and attacks the Doctor's friends.

Hideous Father Christmas face mask and beard disguises creature's true nature

Musical instruments are actually ballistic weapons

Santa suit for camouflage

KILLER CHRISTMAS TREE
The Christmas Tree spins into action. Three sections of the tree spin like buzz-saws as it attacks Rose, Jackie and Mickey. Its leaves are miniature scythes with razor-sharp edges, and it can demolish furniture and even walls. The Doctor manages to stop the tree by using his sonic screwdriver to jam its control signal.

SYCORAX INVASION

While it might seem that the Sycorax and Pilot Fish invaded London at Christmas, the reality was very different. Shooting for *The Christmas Invasion* actually took place in late summer, in Cardiff.

The Sycorax spaceship was a computer-generated image (CGI) added to location footage shot in London and Cardiff. A similar technique was used to create the effect of thousands of people around the world standing ready to jump from various high landmarks. Model work was also used to enhance this – in particular, a model was built of the block of flats where Rose and Jackie live, and the glass was blown out of it for the impressive sequence where the Sycorax spaceship hits the Earth's atmosphere.

SCRIPT EXTRACT

As Rose and Mickey walk (Mickey talking away, oblivious), she's getting a clearer eyeline on the brass band. And something, just instinct, is making Rose concentrate…

Her POV, the angle shifting round, faces becoming visible…
They're all wearing Santa masks. But they're metal. Coloured - rosy cheeks, white beard - but clearly cold, glinting metal. The fixed smile. The sinister jollity.

Rose keeps walking, keeps looking…

Left: The newly regenerated Doctor, and Rose.
Above: Sinister santas attack.

Above (top): Mickey battles a Christmas tree.
Above (bottom): The ship's shockwave shatters glass.

SCRIPT EXTRACT

FX: the tree starts to SPIN! First the bottom third, one
way – the layers of the branches become horizontal discs,
like a giant spinning top – then the middle third spins
the opposite way, then the top third, same direction as
the bottom section. Branches like blades. Spinning fast,
a stack of buzz-saws. The lights are in-built, so they're
a blur of colour as they whip round.

Top: The Sycorax arrive.
Above: A concept painting of the interior of the Sycorax ship.

Right: The fearsome Sycorax.

CREATING THE SYCORAX

Creating the Sycorax was almost like creating two different alien creatures. The costumes were designed by Louise Page, while the masks worn by all the Sycorax warriors were designed and made by Millennium FX, the company also responsible for the Sycorax Leader's prosthetic make-up (including lenses and dentures) and bone-like facial features.

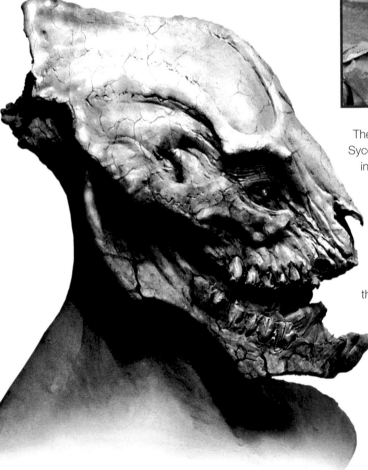

The original idea was to make the Sycorax helmets appear almost medieval in form, so as to match the style of their spaceship. But this was changed when writer and executive producer Russell T Davies explained that he wanted the viewers to assume that the Sycorax helmets were the actual creatures, not masks, so as to increase the impact and surprise when the Sycorax Leader removes his helmet to reveal the terrifying bone-like face beneath. New designs to fit this idea were then modelled as clay miniatures, before the actual masks and make-up elements were created.

Left: The design for the Sycorax leader.
Above: A clay model of the Sycorax helmet.

Top: A design for the Sycorax helmet.
Above: Actor Sean Gilder is made up to become the Sycorax leader.

THE TERILEPTILS

The Terileptils are reptilian bipeds with a love of beauty. They banish their criminals to the planet Raaga, where they toil in the tinclavic mines for the remainder of their lives. A small group of these Terileptil criminals escaped from Raaga. Following his time in the mines, their leader has been left badly scarred around one eye.

The renegades' ship was damaged in an asteroid storm, and only four Terileptils survived the crash-landing on Earth. One was subsequently killed.

Although they can survive in Earth's atmosphere for some time, they use a Soliton gas generator to provide an atmosphere more suitable for Terileptil lungs.

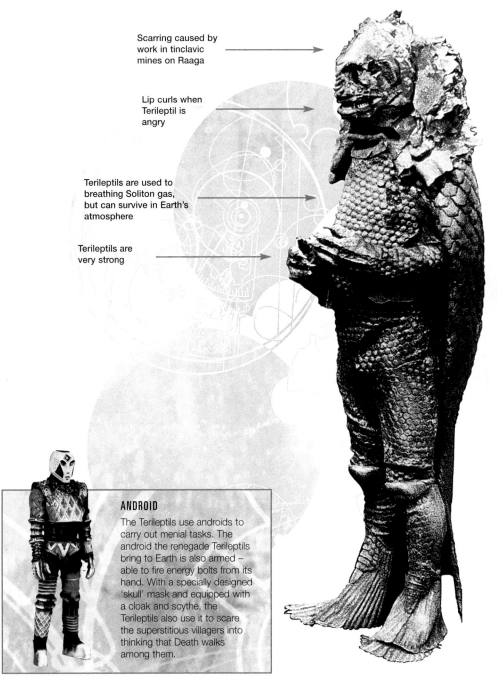

Scarring caused by work in tinclavic mines on Raaga

Lip curls when Terileptil is angry

Terileptils are used to breathing Soliton gas, but can survive in Earth's atmosphere

Terileptils are very strong

ANDROID
The Terileptils use androids to carry out menial tasks. The android the renegade Terileptils bring to Earth is also armed – able to fire energy bolts from its hand. With a specially designed 'skull' mask and equipped with a cloak and scythe, the Terileptils also use it to scare the superstitious villagers into thinking that Death walks among them.

THE VISITATION

Trying to reach present-day Heathrow, the Doctor, Adric, Nyssa and Tegan arrive in the right place, but the wrong time – 1666. Here they meet actor-turned-highwayman Richard Mace, and discover that a small group of aliens has taken over the local manor house.

These Terileptils are escaped convicts who want to rid Earth of humans and take over. Fleeing from villagers under Terileptil mind-control and a Terileptil android dressed as Death, the Doctor and his friends trace the reptiles to London, where they are planning to release a virulent form of the Black Death. The Doctor defeats them at a bakery in Pudding Lane, but in doing so starts a fire…

Written by
Eric Saward
Featuring
the Fifth Doctor, Adric, Nyssa and Tegan
First broadcast
15 February 1982 –
23 February 1982
4 episodes

TERRITORIAL REPTILES

Writer Eric Saward made up the name for the Terileptils by combining 'territorial reptiles'. The script described them as 'about seven feet tall, powerfully built'. Three Terileptil costumes were made for *The Visitation*.

The leader's costume had its face mask sculpted to show scarring round the eye. It's mask was also fitted with electronics to give the face some expression.

MIND CONTROL

The Terileptils can control human minds using special polygrite bracelets with built-in power-packs. The bracelets pulse as the power flows through them. The Terileptil Leader is annoyed that human minds are so primitive that the control is not easy. The Terileptils control various locals, including a poacher, the miller, and the head man of the village. Once the bracelet is removed, the controlled human collapses, and on recovery returns to normal.

PLAGUE

Unable to return home, since they are fugitives, the Terileptils plan to take over Earth by infecting rats with a genetically engineered plague and releasing them to wipe out humanity.

The Terileptil leader has set up a laboratory in the cellar of the local manor house they have taken over, concealed behind a holographic false wall. The other Terileptils have set up a base in the back rooms of a bakery in London, from which to release the rats.

Top: The Terileptil leader confronts the Doctor.

THE WEED CREATURE

The unnamed Weed Creature that attacks the Euro Sea Gas rigs and headquarters is an organism capable of exercising telepathic control. It is part of a colony that derives its intelligence parasitically from the human brains of its hosts, and lives in vast quantities of sea foam. It infects and takes over humans through contact, and emits a toxic gas.

Infected victims begin to grow weed over their skin – unnoticeable at first, but ultimately they will be consumed by the weed.

The Doctor believes the creature has been seen before – in the mid-eighteenth century, by sailors in the North Sea. The creature plans to absorb all human life into its collective colony.

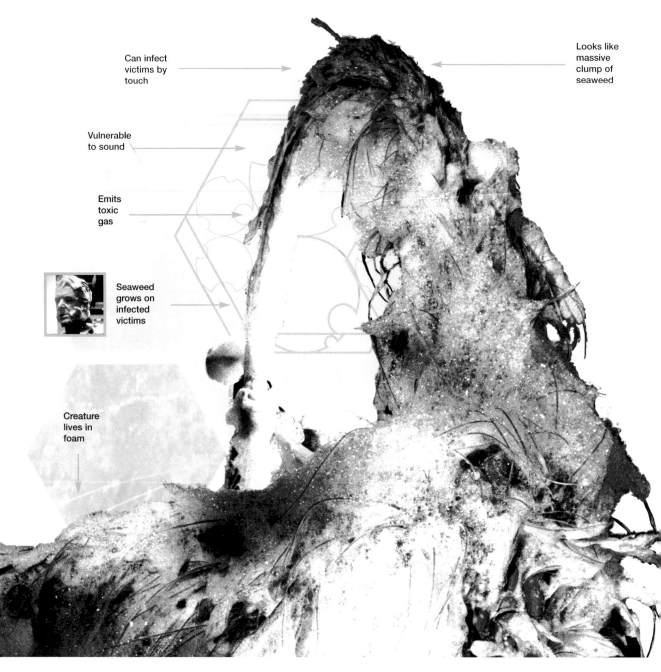

Can infect victims by touch

Looks like massive clump of seaweed

Vulnerable to sound

Emits toxic gas

Seaweed grows on infected victims

Creature lives in foam

Victoria, the Doctor and Jamie by the Euro Sea Gas pipeline.

FURY FROM THE DEEP

The Doctor and his friends arrive at Euro Sea Gas headquarters, where contact has been lost with several gas rigs. The people on the rigs have been infected by a parasitic seaweed. With the Weed Creature infiltrating the headquarters through the gas pipelines and taking over more people, the Doctor flies out to one of the rigs and confronts Chief Robson, head of the complex, and now infected by the seaweed.

The Doctor discovers that the creature is susceptible to noise, having lived in the depths of the sea. He uses the amplified sound of Victoria's screams to destroy it. The Doctor and Jamie are saddened to find that Victoria, tired of endless danger, has decided to stay on Earth.

Written by
Victor Pemberton
Featuring
the Second Doctor,
Jamie and Victoria
First broadcast
16 March 1968 –
20 April 1968
6 episodes

EURO SEA GAS

The Euro Sea Gas complex supplies gas for the whole of Southern England and Wales. Six rigs send gas to a central control rig, which then pumps it ashore through the main pipeline, where the gas is refined.

Buried under the impeller shaft is a vast sealed gasometer. Chief Robson believes that, like an echo chamber, it amplifies the tiniest sound. This is his explanation for the strange 'heartbeat' heard at the rigs and headquarters. But in fact it is the sound made by the Weed Creature as it infests the pipes.

OAK AND QUILL

Oak and Quill were the engineers sent to clear the blockage caused by the Weed Creature, when it was drawn up into the drilling pipes of one of the rigs. They were probably the first people to be infected by the Weed Creature when they came into direct contact with it.

The creature uses the two engineers in its plan to control the Euro Sea Gas complex: they infect Harris by breathing out toxic gas from their mouths. Seaweed grows down their arms and is visible on their hands and at their cuffs. Oak speaks, but Quill always remains silent.

CHIEF ROBSON

Robson is chief of the Euro Sea Gas headquarters and UK operations. He prides himself on the fact that the flow of gas has never been shut off since he took charge. Robson himself spent four years on a rig without a break and has a reputation built on thirty years' experience. The Weed Creature infects Robson, who then kidnaps Victoria and takes her to a seaweed-infested rig.

Once the Weed Creature is destroyed, Robson – along with the other infected people – is returned to normal, with all trace of infection gone.

THE WEED CREATURE

Right: The Weed Creature was a costume worn by an actor, who thrashed about in the foam.
Below: Patrick Troughton, who played the Second Doctor, waits for his cue on the set at the Ealing film studio.

CREATING THE CREATURE

The behind-the-scenes pictures on these pages were taken by resident designer Tony Cornell at the BBC's Ealing Film Studios during the making of *Fury from the Deep*, in 1968. The Weed Creature itself was a suit worn by a member of the visual effects team. By moving his arms and head, he was able to make the creature thrash about in the foam.

Right: The Weed Creature bursts into the control room.

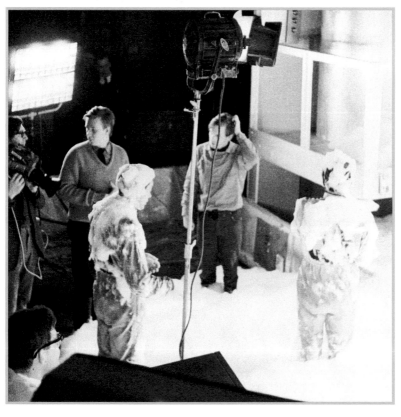

Left: A pause during filming.
Below: The set is flooded with foam ready for the next shot.

THE WEREWOLF

In 1540, something fell to Earth. It landed in the Glen of St Catherine, in Scotland, close to a monastery. Possibly a spore, a virus, or the last remains – the last thought – of some powerful creature from the stars, it survived. It grew, adapted, evolved slowly down the generations until it could take over a human host and live within it. Drawing on local legends and folklore, it mapped itself on the creature at the heart of werewolf legends – a being that turns into a hideous wolf when the moon is full.

Werewolf is immensely strong and savage

Sharp claws can inflict devastating injuries

Human Host becomes a hideous wolf-like creature

Body is covered with thick, matted fur

THE HOST

Once every generation, a child goes missing – and becomes the next Host body for the Werewolf when the existing one has aged and worn out. With its distinctive pure-black eyes and its child-like voice, the Host changes with the full moon into the hideous Werewolf itself.

The current Host was a sickly, local boy, stolen away one night by the Brethren. The creature carved out his soul and sat in his heart.

Rose and the staff of Torchwood House are held captive.

TOOTH AND CLAW

The Doctor and Rose arrive in Scotland in 1879 and meet Queen Victoria, who is on her way to Balmoral. But she is forced to break her journey at Sir Robert MacLeish's house – Torchwood – not knowing that Sir Robert's wife is being held hostage by a group of warrior monks led by the sinister Father Angelo. Followers of an alien life form similar to a traditional werewolf, the monks plan to infect Queen Victoria with the bite of the beast, so that she will become the Host for the alien creature.

The Doctor and Rose help Queen Victoria to escape, and the Doctor puts into action a plan that Sir Robert's father and Queen Victoria's late husband Prince Albert devised to kill the beast using a giant telescope.

Written by
Russell T Davies
Featuring
the Tenth Doctor
and Rose
First broadcast
spring 2006
1 episode

QUEEN VICTORIA

Queen Victoria is 60 years old when she meets the Doctor and Rose. She came to the throne in 1837 and ruled until her death in 1901. Her husband, Prince Albert, died in 1861 and the queen mourned his passing for the rest of her life. What she did not know was that Albert had planned with Sir Robert MacLeish's father to rid the world of the Werewolf that fell to Earth in 1540.

In honour of the plan – and of Sir Robert's sacrifice – Queen Victoria founds the Torchwood Institute to investigate similar strange phenomena.

FATHER ANGELO AND THE BRETHREN

From the monastery in the Glen of St Catherine, the warrior monks led by Father Angelo denounced Sir Robert's father and forbade the villagers to speak to him. They were trying to suppress MacLeish's theories about the creature that fell to Earth close to their monastery.

Followers of the Host, the monks hold Sir Robert's wife hostage and take over his house so as to help the Host infect Queen Victoria. They worship the wolf, chanting: *Lupus magnus est, lupus fortis est, lupus deus est* – 'The wolf is great, the wolf is strong, the wolf is god.'

THE TRAP

Knowing of the local legends, Sir Robert MacLeish's father realised something of the true nature of the Werewolf. Together with Prince Albert, who had knowledge of folklore from his native Germany, he devised a plan to destroy the wolf.

He had a great telescope built at Torchwood House. The plan was to coax the Werewolf into the observatory. As it shied away from the wood panelling varnished with mistletoe oil, it would be destroyed by a powerful beam of moonlight, magnified through the Koh-i-Noor diamond.

Above: The design for the Torchwood Cross.
Right: An actor in a special suit brings the role of the Werewolf to life, to provide positioning information for the creation of the computer-generated images.
Below: The design for the telescope, with the Doctor included for scale.

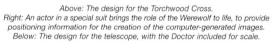

MAKING 'TOOTH AND CLAW'

Above: The initial design for the Werewolf.

For *Tooth and Claw*, as for every other episode of the 2005 and 2006 series of **Doctor Who**, the design was overseen and supervised by production designer Edward Thomas. Each season, the episodes need to have an overall design tone and to include recurring thematic elements, all of which have to be coordinated across the BBC Wales design team and other contributing companies.

For this episode, The Mill was given the responsibility for designing and creating the impressive computer-generated images of the Werewolf itself, and rose to the challenge magnificently. The huge telescope in the Torchwood Observatory was designed by BBC Wales, its pivot system echoing the episode's motif of the moon. The inside of the telescope, seen as the moonlight shines through it, was a model built by the miniature effects team at the Model Unit.

THE WEREWOLF

STORYBOARDING 'TOOTH AND CLAW'

For some sequences in film and television, a series of sketches is produced showing how the action will take place. This is called a storyboard and it is a useful tool for helping the director and the rest of the production team work out and communicate how a sequence should look when finished. The completed storyboard looks rather like a black-and-white cartoon strip, as the sketches below show.

While many sequences, particularly those involving effects and computer imagery, have been storyboarded for **Doctor Who** before, *Tooth and Claw* was the first episode for which storyboards were produced for the majority of the action.

The examples reproduced here show just how much care and attention was put into planning every aspect of the production.

The storyboard for the opening sequence, in which the monks arrive at Torchwood House and do battle with the Steward and the stablehands.

Inhabitants of the now-barren planet of Vortis, the Zarbi are a giant cross between ants and beetles, controlled by the power of the Animus. They are not intelligent, and lived at peace with the other inhabitants of Vortis until they were made militant by the dark power of the Animus. But even aliens are scared of spiders: the Zarbi react with fear to a dead specimen the Doctor has, presumably perceiving a similarity with the Animus that controls them.

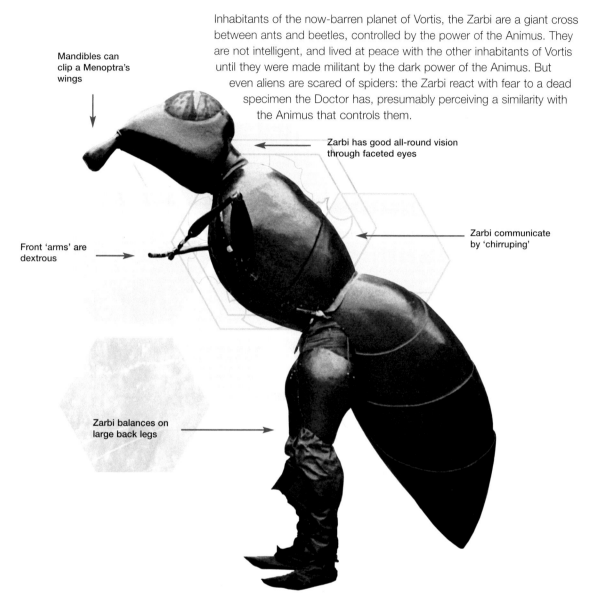

Mandibles can clip a Menoptra's wings

Zarbi has good all-round vision through faceted eyes

Front 'arms' are dextrous

Zarbi communicate by 'chirruping'

Zarbi balances on large back legs

THE ANIMUS

The Animus is a parasitic being hidden at the heart of a fungus-like web-city known as the Carsenome, which has appeared on the surface of the planet Vortis, centred over its magnetic pole and drawing out the power of the planet itself. The Animus's malevolent influence has destroyed the flower forest that used to cover Vortis. A cross between a spider and an octopus, the Animus controls the Zarbi and their Larvae Guns, and has turned them against the peaceful Menoptra and driven them away. It can also control anyone in contact with gold.

The Carsenome web city uses vegetation to grow – the vegetation is fed into acid pools by the prisoners at the Crater of Needles, then drawn through underground streams to the central roots of the city.

A Zarbi waits by the TARDIS on the barren planet of Vortis.

THE WEB PLANET

Written by
Bill Strutton
Featuring
the First Doctor, Ian, Barbara and Vicki
First broadcast
13 February 1965 – 20 March 1965
6 episodes

The TARDIS is drawn to the barren planet Vortis, where the Animus controls the ant-like Zarbi, who have expelled the native Menoptra. Now the Menoptra are ready to return to Vortis and destroy the Animus. But the Doctor and Vicki are captured by the Zarbi and forced to discover the Menoptra's plans, while Barbara is made to work with captured Menoptra in the Crater of Needles.

Despite their initial attack force being all-but wiped out, the surviving Menoptra join forces with the Doctor and his friends and fight their way to the Animus, where it is destroyed with a special isoptope – a living destructor that reverses the growth process, causing cells to die.

VENOM GRUBS

Also known as 'Larvae Guns', the venom grubs have an armoured shell and move on many thin legs, a bit like a woodlouse. Their long proboscises can fire a bolt of energy, powerful enough to kill Menoptra and to blast through the walls of the Carsenome.

Only the Zarbi can control them, but whether the grubs develop into Zarbi or a completely different species when they reach adulthood is not known.

THE MENOPTRA

Like giant butterflies, the Menoptra are the intelligent natives of the planet Vortis. Despite the thin atmosphere, they have the power of flight. They move in a stylised manner and gesticulate with their fingerless hands while talking. Their speech is accented and shrill, and they are unable to pronounce the names of the travellers – so Ian, for example, becomes 'Heron' while Barbara is 'Harbara'. Before the Animus arrived, the Menoptra lived in harmony with the Zarbi and other creatures. They worshipped light and built beautiful temples.

THE OPTERA

Eight-legged caterpillar-like creatures, the Optera live underground. They use crystal shards for weapons. They call the Animus 'Pwodarauk', and their language is an amalgam of both surface and underground ideas and images – stalagmites are 'trees of stone'. Hetra, the leader, describes 'making mouths' in a 'silent wall' when talking of digging.

The Optera do not remember that they were once Menoptra, whom they now regard as their gods.

CREATING THE ZARBI

The many monsters and aliens that have appeared on **Doctor Who** were created by the various BBC design departments. For the original 'classic' series, design was almost always carried out in-house at the BBC. Today, design work is shared between various BBC design departments and outside companies, overseen by production designer Edward Thomas.

In the 1960s, 1970s and 1980s, whether a creature was designed by the scenic designer or the costume designer, or realised through make-up, depended on the script as well as the skills of the people involved.

Generally, Scenic Design was responsible for 'props' – like the Daleks and the Zarbi – and Costume Design for costumes that were 'worn' by an actor (like the Menoptra), but there was considerable overlap. The creatures that inhabited the Web Planet were a collaboration of the various departments; the Zarbi themselves were designed by BBC designer John Wood, and then built mainly from fibreglass by an outside company called Shawcraft Models – the same company that made the original Daleks from Raymond P. Cusick's designs.

From the time of the Second Doctor onwards, the BBC's visual effects department was also involved and often provided design and/or realisation of part of a creature – such as the 'hands' or components of the costume.

As with the programme as a whole, the creatures of **Doctor Who** are a collaborative effort that showcases the expertise of the BBC design departments and outside companies, and the talents of the people who work in them.

Top: The final touches are added to a Zarbi costume at Shawcraft Models.
Right: Scenic designer John Wood's initial design for the Zarbi.